PRAISE FOR

THE BUSINESS OF AMBIGUITY

"In combining academic theory of organizational psychology with actual people and situations, the author brings to life the challenges faced in addressing uncertainty, complexity, and imperfect information. This is an invaluable business guide for the world in which we now live."

—DEBORAH HAZELL, CEO of Unity Trust Bank and
nonexecutive director of Global Parametrics

"In corporate life, the ability to see around corners, to anticipate what bad (or good) thing may happen next, is a precious and rare attribute. As Debbie Sutherland eloquently argues in this essential book, we are all a product of our personal experiences; we all learn to deal with ambiguity through our values, behaviors, and mindsets. If COVID-19 has demonstrated one thing to those in corporate life, it's that constancy, the steadfastness of mind under duress, predictability, and anticipation are at least as mission critical as technical capabilities. This is a vital body of work for these times, allowing the successful executive to embrace and thrive amid so much ambiguity."

—ED SIMS, president and CEO of WestJet Airlines

"This book is a solid read for leaders at all levels. It's timely and offers practical suggestions and thoughtful insights on what and how to make decisions when faced with ambiguity. Debbie Sutherland offers the reader a comprehensive journey through adult learning theory, systems thinking, and multiple constructs, supported by relevant, real-world examples."

—JULIA SLOAN, author of *Learning to Think Strategically*
and president of Sloan International

"Whether or not we live in a world of increasing ambiguity is not something we can control; how we respond to ambiguity, on the other hand, is entirely up to us. In this fascinating and well-referenced investigation into the inner workings of our minds, Debbie Sutherland introduces us to ourselves in ways that can be both challenging and beneficial. Regardless of our profession, if we could put to use even 10 percent of the advice that Sutherland offers based on her interviews and observations of executives, our response to ambiguous situations would be improved dramatically, as would our success."

—BILL PASMORE, PhD, professor of practice of social-organizational psychology at Teachers College, Columbia University, senior vice president of the Center for Creative Leadership, and author of *Advanced Consulting*

DR. DEBBIE SUTHERLAND

The
BUSINESS
of
AMBIGUITY

Demystify the Unknown with Five Key
Thinking and Behavior Strategies

RIVER GROVE
BOOKS

Published by River Grove Books
Austin, TX
www.rivergrovebooks.com

Distributed by River Grove Books

Design and composition by Greenleaf Book Group and Teresa Muñiz
Cover design by Greenleaf Book Group and Teresa Muñiz
Cover image used under license from ©Shutterstock/Kitsana1980

Publisher's Cataloging-in-Publication data is available.

Print ISBN: 978-1-63299-461-5

eBook ISBN: 978-1-63299-462-2

· First Edition

CONTENTS

Foreword vii

Preface xi

Introduction:
 The Ambiguity Mindset 1

Chapter 1:
 Create Powerful Insights through Critical Reflection 23

Chapter 2:
 Cultivate Adaptable Mental Models. 49

Chapter 3:
 Develop Comfort in the Unknown 75

Chapter 4:
 Learn through Person, Context, and Environment 99

Chapter 5:
 Harness the Strategic Power of Diverse Networks. 123

Chapter 6:
 Your Leadership Legacy 143

Acknowledgments 155

Appendix A:
 Dealing with Ambiguity: A Self-Assessment
 Questionnaire. 157

Appendix B:
 Critical Reflection Journal Prompts 159

Appendix C:

My Dinner Party. 161

Appendix D:

Comprehensive Review Chart 163

Appendix E:

Ambiguity Mindset Model 165

References 167

Index 173

About the Author. 181

FOREWORD

The popularly of the acronym VUCA (volatility, uncertainty, complexity, and ambiguity) reflects the relevancy of The Business of Ambiguity for people living in the twenty-first century. Contemporary challenges, being driven by innovations in technologies, are confronting organizations, functions and groups within organizations, and individuals alike. Of course, ambiguity has always been a part of life; the future has never been totally predictable. But now that we have entered the age of 4.0, the so-called Fourth Industrial Revolution, the pace of change has accelerated the increasing complexity of the changes confronting people.

What appears to be a strategic path for organizations or people can be suddenly uprooted, requiring reorganization, restaffing, or reskilling. This necessitates that leaders, and people in general, are able to anticipate disruptions and develop their capacity for navigating through the ambiguity that is inherent in these ongoing challenges so they can constructively leverage the potential benefits and insights that emerge. It is important to note that while the ambiguity that confronts people is often related to what the future holds, ambiguity also exists in the present, in current situations in which the dynamics are uncertain, such as an important meeting in which people's thoughts are not clear.

In either case, acting effectively entails having the capacity for *learning through* ambiguity as it is unfolding. The process of *learning through* requires you to be aware of how you are experiencing the ambiguity and to skillfully apply learning practices that will enable you to effectively navigate the process.

It is also important to become aware of any biases you have that are shaping your perceptions of the situation. Doing this involves developing what Dr. Debbie Sutherland calls an ambiguity mindset. This book does more than share information and knowledge; it provides a guide for engaging in a process of personal learning that enables the development of this mindset. The process and practices provided here are based on Dr. Sutherland's research and her extensive experience working globally with executives in the application of systematic organizational change and talent management.

The chapters take us through the five key thinking and behavior strategies for developing an ambiguity mindset. The process begins with engaging in personal reflection, something that is foundational for developmental learning but often not engaged in by many people. Reflection is at the core of cultivating the adaptive mental models necessary for navigating ambiguity and developing comfort with being in the unknown. This comfort enables you to learn from your interactions within the uncertain context. Furthermore, leveraging the diverse networks available to you, particularly those that you are not initially comfortable interacting within, provides pathways to new insights for moving forward. In short, this book provides a sequence of development for learning your way through ambiguity.

While the book is based on adult learning theory, it is about personal engagement in the practice, not just becoming more familiar with theory. Each chapter provides reflective questions for personal assessment; it is engaging with these questions that provides the most valuable learning and development.

In many ways this book is a guide through a process of learning and development that Dr. Sutherland has experienced herself. The personal experiences she shares not only illustrate her points but also provide a basis for thinking about similar situations you have encountered. As you connect the experiences shared in the book with your own experiences, it is useful to reflect on what assumptions you were holding, how the practices in this book could have been applied, and you what might have done differently. This exercise fosters a way of being in the world that enhances your comfort with ambiguity and ability to learn through it.

Getting the full benefit of the knowledge presented here involves not just reading the book but continuing to revisit the ideas and learn through ambiguity by applying the practices. I encourage you to engage in these practices and, when leading others, construct environments that facilitate their development, to enable working through the ambiguity confronting the group as well.

Enjoy the journey.

—LYLE YORKS, *professor of the Adult Learning and Leadership Program, Teachers College, Columbia University*

PREFACE

The path of least resistance and least trouble is a mental
rut already made. It requires troublesome work to
undertake the alteration of old beliefs.
—JOHN DEWEY, *How We Think*

Have you ever been faced with a puzzling pattern of events, been stuck in a confusing situation, or felt trapped by your own routine thinking patterns? Confused about how to navigate through difficult workplace behaviors? Have you ever wondered about how you think and make decisions during ambiguous or uncertain situations? What is your ambiguity story?

Imagine that the executive team of an international shipping company has asked you to help build a new shipping port in a foreign country. As a seasoned senior manager who has studied port design and technology, you are confident you can lead the design and start-up operations, even though this is your first international assignment. You are an expert in marine shipping strategies such as international pricing and trade agreements to leverage better access to trade channels. You love adventure, so the assignment is perfect for the next step in your career.

You eagerly agree to the challenge, and within three months, you have moved your family to a small town in Malaysia and placed your two children into an international school, but you wonder about the outdoor classrooms and the dense forest full of unfamiliar creatures less than a mile from the playground. Your new villa is not typical, as it has an outdoor kitchen, and your meals are now filled with unusual tastes and smells. This new environment adds ambiguity to your daily life, complicating all of your decisions at home and at work.

On the job, you quickly realize that all your work experiences and education have not prepared you for the sheer confusion and uncertainty that you are now experiencing every day. Reporting to the Malaysian CEO, you are now responsible for more general management of people and resources, team management skills you have never dealt with. Shipping laborers are nonexistent in the small town, so you must travel up and down the coast to negotiate and persuade the farmers to learn new skills and become ship workers. You quickly become exhausted from the language barrier and nontraditional ways of doing business. You begin to think that you may fail in your first overseas assignment.

Alternatively, picture yourself as the VP of Renewable Energy who landed a job in the United Arab Emirates (UAE) and is tasked with building a renewable energy project. The mandate is steeped in unknowns. The economics are against the project, as there are limited government renewable energy policies in place. The company has five different operating business models and interacts frequently with foreign ministers, conglomerates, and scientists. New technologies are being developed every year, and each department is focused on its own ever-changing agendas, stakeholders, and ambitious targets.

With so many external forces potentially disrupting the corporate strategy, how can the company create a business plan for five or even three years in advance? How can you forecast during this type of environmental and economic ambiguity? You also have no experience living or working in the Middle East and wonder if you will be able to understand the dynamics of the project, people, and culture well enough to launch this project.

CONFRONTING AMBIGUITY

Consider this: People don't hate change; they hate ambiguity. People may be more uncomfortable with the feeling of not knowing—with ambiguous situations—rather than with the thought of change itself. But what does ambiguity mean?

Ambiguity is when the nature of a problem is itself in question, information is unreliable, goals are unclear or conflicting, contradictions and paradoxes appear, and cause-and-effect relationships are poorly understood. Essentially, ambiguity refers to confusing probabilities and uncertainty from imperfect or unknown information. Over the years, I have seen firsthand how executives differ widely in their understanding of and comfort level on an ambiguity spectrum. Some executives are on one side of the spectrum and avoid ambiguity and the cognitive stress that uncertainty brings. They ignore nuances when faced with too many opportunity streams and simply make fast, decisive decisions or feel anxious when they can't see which path is better; sometimes they stall decision-making until they get more information. Conversely, on the other side of the spectrum, some executives build a tolerance for ambiguous situations by learning different coping mechanisms.

Knowing that ambiguity means different things to different executives and that uncertain situations often prevail in businesses, many forward-thinking companies have developed considerable interest in understanding how executives can learn the nuances of cognitive complexities, including how adult learning, systems thinking, and organizational behavior theories can help develop an ambiguity mindset.

You have no doubt encountered a situation of ambiguity in which your assumptions are challenged, then your thinking becomes clearer, and at last you finally get it and are able to see through the mental roadblocks. My moment occurred during a weekend in New York City while attending an event called a *group relations conference*. To become full-fledged organizational psychologists, the attendees were informed by the esteemed Debra A. Noumair, professor of psychology and education at Columbia University and key maestro for creating the systems psychodynamics and organizational change executive education program, that all three of Columbia University's organizational psychology master's cohorts were required to attend the conference. We had heard rumors—bad rumors—that we would learn things that would shake us to our core. And it was true; I was a different person after the conference.

It was not a typical conference, as this event involved "learning from experience" methods to uncover group and social dynamics; to explore the undercurrent of social behaviors, assumptions, and cultural norms; and to understand how authority and power are used consciously and unconsciously in groups. I knew things would be different as soon as I entered the large conference room; rather than facing forward as usual, all the seats were placed in a circle facing inward.

The conference started when the facilitator, a faculty member of the Organizational Psychology Department, placed a chair in the center of the room, sat down, and asked us to begin the task.

Confusion set in immediately. After about two minutes, which felt like an eternity, someone shyly asked, "What is the task?"

The facilitator remained silent, which felt unsettling and

uncomfortable. You could see a few people across the room whispering, but no one spoke up.

Eventually, one person stated, "There is no task. We need to decide what the task is."

At this moment, one of the West Point officers, who was attending as part of his master's degree for military training, stood up with some display of authority and stated that we should elect a leader of the group and volunteered himself to facilitate a discussion. Apparently, someone did not agree and rudely asked him to sit down. I whispered to a colleague one of the most taboo statements you can make in my profession. I said, "I hate groups."

To my surprise, my friend whispered back, "Me too."

Shortly after the West Point officer's awkward moment, someone thought we should move our chairs closer to the center, as it would be easier to have a conversation. Eager for something to happen, about thirty people moved their chairs closer together. And then nothing. Sensing that the facilitator's role was to remain silent, we came to the realization that we were in charge of both nothing and everything. Yet, after another thirty minutes, we were still arguing about what we should talk about. It seemed that learning how to navigate confusion, tension, and friction through debate in a larger group had begun.

Recollecting that one of the goals of the conference was to understand power and authority in large groups, I began to understand that each time someone spoke up, stood up, or gave a strong opinion, it was an action—conscious or unconscious—of someone trying to seize power and exert authority to test their hidden insecurities. While the book *Lean In* by Sheryl Sandberg, chief operating officer at Facebook, had not been published yet, I was aware that I should speak up at least once, so I staked my claim of power for five seconds by adding my voice to the tense discussion; thankfully, nobody told me to sit down.

I could now retreat to my comfort zone as an observer. Interestingly, the discussion pivoted toward the facilitator still in the middle of the room, who was accused of showing his real power and authority by being silent.

At this point, I knew why I disliked groups; the deep-seated assumptions, biases, and perspectives are hidden—until they aren't. I was amazed how each smart and talented business, military, and education expert's behavior changed so quickly when faced with their own insecurities.

After lunch, I was assigned to a small group of six people, and we had a different faculty member guiding us on a new task. We were asked the same question: What did we want the task to be? However, it was now easier, as we all wanted to discuss what had happened in the morning session. We collectively observed the following:

- It is difficult to problem solve and acknowledge different perspectives in large groups.

- The proximity of the chairs changed the dynamics in the room, as some people felt more secure in the outer edge, while other people felt more secure when seated in a tighter group.

- We observed the numerous times that power and authority were tossed to different people but that no one sustained the power for long.

- There was a lack of patience to listen to anyone for any length of time, as it was difficult to articulate more than one thought before someone would interrupt with a new thought.

- Unless someone is assigned a role in a large group, we tend to take the role we are most comfortable with, such as observer, leader, team player, peacemaker, or problem solver.

We have enough leadership research to understand that leaders are not born but rather are developed over time. The illusive leadership capacity is built on a series of uncomfortable learning moments, events, and experiences, and in that situation, we were all witnessing leaders in the making. We were exposing ourselves to rejection, verbal attack, bias, and isolation while embarking on the difficult process of reflecting on those embarrassing moments.

A crucial aspect of experiential learning is that it is important to be present in the here and now to interact with the undercurrents of covert and overt behaviors but also to reflect on all those complex behaviors on display within the group. By the end of the day, everyone was exhausted and had a lot to think about in terms of understanding power and authority in group dynamics.

On day 2, everyone was asked to form their own groups and create a theme for a group discussion. I joined a group of five women from different nationalities, and we quickly agreed we should explore our international cultural experiences. This group turned out to be an interesting and safe haven from the trauma experienced in the large group session.

Interestingly, not all the self-selecting groups had the same experience. Thirteen people decided to become a group and call themselves the Alphas. As you can expect, the Alphas could not agree on a team task, and two people, who were still frustrated from the large group session on day 1, decided not to do a damn thing for the rest of the day and headed off to the nearby college pub, while the rest of the group sat on the floor and chatted all day. The behavior of this group was a textbook example of Tuckman's theory of teams, in which there are five phases: forming, storming, norming, performing, and adjourning. The "Splinter Alpha" group, which we now called them, stayed in the forming and storming phases for the entire conference and never made it to the norming phase.

THINKING AND BEHAVIOR INSIGHTS

The takeaway from the entire conference was a deep and meaningful understanding of group dynamics as played out in a type of *Lord of the Flies* or *Hunger Games* situation. We were immersed in one another's identity, perspectives, experiences, and differences, and, of course, all the uncomfortable discussions regarding trust, power, authority, and biases. As organizational psychologists who were being trained to become the corporate experts on change management, we had successfully completed the painful and humbling experiential learning exercise, which proved that even the employees who want to assist in corporate change may somehow—consciously or unconsciously—sabotage the task.

My own stunning learning moments? I had strong feelings of anger, distrust, and vulnerability, which I don't usually feel. I was amazed at the fluid and dynamic ways that different perspectives and assumptions were rudely disregarded by some smart, forward-thinking people. I was also perplexed about how the Splinter Alpha group was unable to see what was happening within their own dynamics and behaviors. However, the ultimate takeaway from the conference was my ability to embrace teams and the complexity of behaviors and thinking patterns group members exhibit when faced with ambiguity and uncertainty. I honestly felt that I could now see dysfunctional groups with a sort of X-ray vision revealing the unique unconscious behaviors that interfered in their progress.

WHAT WERE WE THINKING?

In learning about group dynamics at that conference, my desire to understand how other people think and act during times of ambiguity deepened. Moving forward in my career, I continued to wonder about the misunderstandings, paradoxes, and unintentional acts that unfold regularly throughout our lives. I was curious about what each of us was thinking that got us to this place.

I knew that my future professional interests were going to be in analyzing behaviors and chaotic situations. And as I began to learn more about adult learning and development during my doctoral research, I had even more questions: What propels some people to be able to see an ill-defined decision-making path better than others? Why are some people more comfortable working in ambiguous situations, while other people react negatively?

As I continued to work overseas with diverse executives, I also noticed that some executives, who had no formal training in systems dynamics, decision sciences, or chaos theories, were able to navigate the complexity and nuances of business dynamics with greater success than others. I wanted to know the executives' thinking and behavior patterns; I wanted to know how they learned this skill, and what elements helped them make good decisions when they encountered situations they'd never experienced before.

MEET THE EXECUTIVES

Exploring ambiguous situations within the UAE is ideal, as this small nation is one of the most developed countries in the Arab Gulf. This country is making huge investments in tourism, technology, manufacturing, and construction and was ranked twenty-fifth of 141 countries on the global competitive index for 2019 (World Economic Forum, 2019). This situation of economic growth and diversity creates both challenges and opportunities on how to manage the increasingly complex global market, and executives who work in these types of environments must be able to address the dynamic and instantaneous changes that arise.

To gain an understanding of the thinking and behavior patterns of those working in conditions of ambiguity, I met with dozens of top-level executives working in the UAE who were operating in business, academia, and government sectors and held titles such as CEO, managing director, advisor, or president. These executives were selected, as they were the key decision makers operating within dynamic domains that were deemed adaptive and evolving in a changing landscape. Furthermore, each executive is considered influential, prominent, and well informed. The selected executives also have twenty-plus years of experience within dynamic organizations that have multiple stakeholders, multiple business models, connections to joint ventures and partnerships, or frequent interactions with external influences.

The executives were selected from different domains—such as oil and gas, health care, shipping, hospitality, transportation, information and technology, academia, real estate development, private equity, education, entrepreneurship, conglomerate, and renewable energy—and represent different genders and nationalities, such as Lebanese, Dutch, American, British, Italian, Australian, and Emirati. In this book, I share their ambiguity learning insights with you.

THREE KEY QUESTIONS

Drawing on my education in adult learning and organizational psychology, my interest in systems thinking, and my observations of business behavior patterns, I created three main research questions, which will guide you through the rest of this book:

- What are the beliefs, behaviors, and principles of business executives who work in conditions of ambiguity?

- What experiences and events provide the scaffolding in the development of an ambiguity mindset?

- What relationships, systems, and elements in the environment enable executives to develop an ambiguity thinking capacity?

Through an analysis of the interviews, focus groups, and academic theories, my results showed how these executives learned to make dynamic decisions in times of uncertainty by relying on the same five key thinking and behavior strategies, which are the key components of an ambiguity mindset.

TURNING INFORMATION INTO WISDOM

The prime objective of the ambiguity mindset is to build a whole new perspective on how to think and act when you face a lack of information, conflicting agendas, or uncertain direction. This book explores the three main decoding principles—learn to view the world through a wide-angle lens to gain perspective-taking skills, learn the components of your behavior and thinking architecture, and learn within different environments.

Each chapter takes you on a deep dive into the five ambiguity thinking and behavior strategies. You will learn about the research, tools, and resources that are the underpinning of each strategy. You will learn from the executives' real stories how they developed the capacity to understand ambiguous situations with greater clarity. Understanding how the concepts overlap and are interrelated will help you comprehend how to build these thinking and behavior strategies into your personal and professional decision-making portfolio.

Learning the ambiguity mindset theory is the first step toward applying it in your own setting. The book contains learning insights and exercises that will help you build new thinking and behavioral habits. However, learning requires action. Reading a recipe does not make you a good cook; you have to actually cook. You must embrace the power of behavioral practice before your actions can create measurable positive outcomes.

I am thrilled to share my insights with you on how to understand ambiguous situations. You'll learn more about your own and other people's thinking and behavior patterns when faced with ambiguity and uncertainty. You'll develop ways to avoid routine thinking habits and seek deeper understanding of the biases and assumptions that affect your decisions. Leveraging your ability to build high-performance teams, you will understand the conditions that will empower others to build an ambiguity mindset. You will increase your ability to lead within uncertain situations and learn how to build strategic learning pathways for insightful change.

My hope is that this book provides a strategic path toward learning more about the business behaviors and thinking patterns that will help you manage the amazing—and messy—world we live in.

. . . . .

THE AMBIGUITY MINDSET

Knowledge gaps are our reality. We live in a dynamic and interconnected world, and making well-informed and long-term decisions has become progressively difficult, given our limited understanding of the basis of unanticipated events or unintended business consequences. As this complexity increases, patterns of error and system-wide problems become more difficult to predict, and even our new technologies and interconnectedness continue to complicate global businesses. Ambiguous situations are now normal for global companies, and executives must constantly struggle with that uncertainty to make informed decisions.

The issues are compounded, as even highly educated executives may struggle with the pace of change. Each project comes with unique demands, and the pathway through ambiguous situations has no pre-defined learning path. Executives need to make leadership decisions in real time for maximum efficiency. Organizations also have many different types of corporate and personal relationships, which are a melting pot of behaviors, emotions, and attitudes that can invoke feelings of anxiety, confusion, or conflict. So how do you absorb, manage, or mitigate all these business uncertainties while still making good business decisions?

The ambiguity mindset is the cognitive and behavioral capacity to reflect on, examine, and adapt perspectives and to seek meaning from dynamic connections, interactions, experiences, and behaviors to determine the ideal decision pathway. It is a thinking and behavioral action mindset that enables you to make good decisions. The ambiguity mindset is a way of addressing cognitive complexities and behavioral insights and a way of learning how to think and act while immersed in unfamiliar situations. Systems thinking, adult learning, and organizational behavior theories provide insights into the nuances of business uncertainty to decode the key principles.

The purpose of an ambiguity mindset is to learn how to embrace the components of ambiguous situations, dive into why ambiguous situations occur, and learn to see and appreciate the nuances with better clarity. Developing an ambiguity mindset is a multifaceted and multilevel process that will enable you to understand the behavior patterns, relationships, inferences, and perceptions within the network of systems to avoid unintended business consequences. You must learn this intellectual thinking competency and avoid linear thinking within layers of systems; you also must transform wisdom into dynamic actions and understand cause-and-effect relationships necessary to solve recurring or systemic issues. To do this, you must self-reflect on faulty biases and assumptions you may hold so you can understand the true nature of ambiguity.

The ambiguity mindset journey will help you embrace a new way of thinking. Its foundation is framed by the main decoding principles and includes four concepts that are also part of an ambiguity mindset:

mental models, systems thinking, complex adaptive systems, and learning from experience.

DECODING PRINCIPLES

The first decoding principle is to view the world through a wide-angle lens. You will learn the value of gaining perspective-taking skills. This big-picture decoding principle explains how your own perspective can expand to capture more clues for broader understanding. Learning about your own and other people's thinking patterns is the first step toward understanding your blind spots, assumptions, and biases so you can see the world through multiple viewpoints.

The second decoding principle builds a behavior and thinking architecture for an ambiguity mental model. Even with no prior knowledge of systems thinking, you will learn the systems thinking foundation and become more familiar with sophisticated terminology such as feedback loops, dynamic interactions, and unintended consequences, as well as the repercussions of short-term thinking. The fact is that you are a product of your upbringing, which created your personal values; you have learned experiences from the context of situations around you. But the rule of this decoding principle is that you need to see all the elements in the fluid and dynamic system you live in. By understanding more about your own and other people's thinking and behavior patterns, you will move away from introspection and into the outer spheres—the organizational and environmental space—and start to build skills to understand why context matters. You will then be able to switch between *self* and *others* and will learn to ask key questions that build the connections in all three macro spheres: individual, organization, and environment.

The third decoding principle is based on the different experiences and the environments in which you learn. The fact is that we all learn differently, and adults learn differently than children. More than likely, you have not thought about how you learn or how you think while working in unfamiliar situations with different groups of people—specifically, in complex adaptive systems. This decoding principle will enable you to seek meaning in your situational experiences and build communities and networks to create new learning pathways.

The three decoding principles help build the ambiguity mindset foundation and enable you to understand inexactness, paradoxes, or uncertain situations (ambiguity) within the business context (principles, behaviors, and knowledge-making architecture) and the ideal conditions (influencers, elements, interactions, and experiences) to develop an ambiguity mindset. Now, let's dive into the four main concepts of an ambiguity mindset and how you can start to visualize your thinking and behavior actions in different spheres of insight. All of these components build the foundation for your strategic learning path.

SPHERES OF INSIGHT

Urie Bronfenbrenner—professor of human development and psychology at Cornell University and widely regarded as one of the world's leading scholars in developmental psychology, child-rearing, and human ecology—developed the ecological systems theory to explore the five levels that can influence human development: the microsystem, the mesosystem, the exosystem, the macrosystem, and the chronosystem (Bronfenbrenner, 1994).

Bronfenbrenner believed that a child's development was affected by everything in his or her surrounding environment and the combination of experiences and knowledge gained. The ecological systems theory research helped explain how two siblings living in the same family and living situation (microsystem and mesosystem) can develop differently and can have different views of their childhood from their varied experiences and interactions through their activities and relationships: the neighbors, friends, and city cultural influences (exosystem, macrosystems, and chronosystem). For example, if one of the siblings took music lessons or participated on a sports team while the other sibling was bullied by the neighborhood kids, their childhood experiences will have diverged, and they may have different perceptions of their childhoods. This model helped educators understand that students learn differently based on their own lived experiences and that each lived experience helped develop their understanding of their world (Bronfenbrenner, 1994). Bronfenbrenner's development ecology model (as illustrated in Niederer et al., 2009) explains how an immediate situation has many different influencers as it interacts with the environment (see Figure 1).

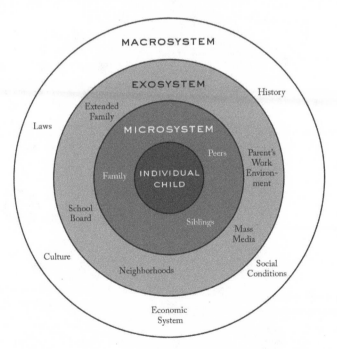

FIGURE 1. BRONFENBRENNER'S ECOLOGICAL MODEL
(SOURCE: NIEDERER ET AL., 2009)

Similarly, the ambiguity mindset model is a visual representation and links the spheres of insight to the individual, organizational, and environmental perspectives as a set of nested structures but with an open system to showcase how the environment continually affects your perceptions and experiences. The ambiguity mindset model takes into account the interrelationships and multilayered structure and includes the main theories—systems thinking, adult learning, and organizational behaviors—in the outer sphere and the key concepts and the five thinking and behavior strategies in the inner connected area. Figure 2 is an illustration of all the components of an ambiguity mindset. (This illustration also appears in Appendix E for quick reference.)

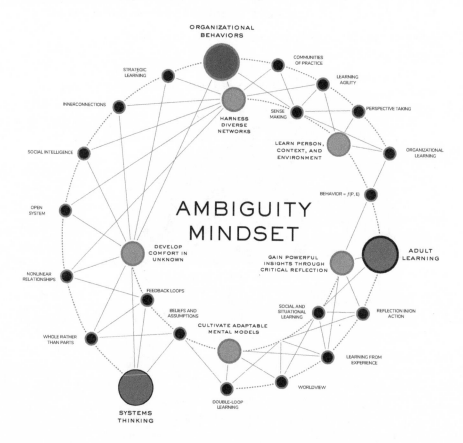

FIGURE 2. AMBIGUITY MINDSET MODEL

MENTAL MODELS

I suspect that people may ask you every day for your opinion on a variety of topics. However, have you ever thought about how you think or what thinking patterns or mental models you rely on?

Mental models are essentially the beliefs, attitudes, or cognitive frameworks that you use to understand the world, make assumptions, create knowledge, and shape your perspectives. Understanding your mental models is vital for understanding ambiguity, because your experiences and how you seek to understand them will frame your perspectives. Robert Kegan, a Harvard University professor, stated that mental models are developed through a lifetime of experiences that shape and develop behavior patterns and actions that guide people within different situations, events, and environments (Kegan, 1994). However, mental models are not fixed. They can be expanded but frequently become entrenched in narrow thinking pathways and can limit creative thinking options.

Let's begin to explore your thinking patterns. Do you usually jump into situations without a plan? Or do you try to organize each detail before you feel comfortable enough to execute on the plan? Or are you one of those people who just lets the experiences happen around you?

As you self-reflect, it might become evident that your past experiences will have taught you which scenarios created the best outcome for you and your expectations. If the scenarios had a positive outcome, you probably began to conduct the same type of thinking for future scenarios.

Try this: Reflect back on your high school study habits. Have you ever crammed for a test or forgotten about a project due date and stayed up all night to meet the deadline, and then ended up with a good grade? This result may have surprised you, and you may even have considered yourself lucky. Even so, you more than likely tried this practice again to test the theory that cramming for a test still enabled you to receive good results. Therefore, this type of thinking became your mental model or thinking pattern. Of course, if cramming for a test or leaving critical project details to the last moment was unsuccessful for you and you received a bad grade, you learned how to build time into your next work requirement, and that became your thinking pattern for future exams.

But was it your thinking patterns that got you through the unfamiliar situation, or was it the happenstance of the elements around you that solved the problem? It may have been a bit of both. You may have successfully passed the test because of the last-minute studying and, unknown to you, the teacher decided to increase the class test scores and made an easy test. Does this new information change your mental model at how successful you were at cramming for that test?

When faced with similar situations, you can tap into your memory and find a similar experience to assist with decision-making. However, when faced with a paradox or ambiguity, it is not easy to make decisions, as your mind may not have enough experiences to make an informed decision. Additionally, you may also make strong assumptions or rely on your biases, such as confirmation bias, which is the tendency to process information by looking for an example that is already consistent with your beliefs. So how do you make informed decisions when faced with unique situations and some ambiguity? You must start by taking a deep dive into your own thoughts (or metacognition) to find clues on how you think and react in uncertain situations.

LEARNING INSIGHT

• • • • •

Think of a time when you were surprised at new information that changed your previously held strong belief or principle. What was your thinking and behavior regarding the issue?

SYSTEMS THINKING

You are integrated into various systems, whether you realize it or not: your family, communities, organizations, clubs, or teams. Each of these systems interacts in complex ways. Try counting the number of systems you interact with, and you can begin to see why people have difficulty creating a work-life balance. The term *work-life balance* is a misnomer, as it is not a duality concept. Instead, it reflects more than that; it's about living in a network of dynamic, constantly changing, and adaptive systems. The concept of systems thinking enables you to explore how the world works, how its systems interact, and how you interact within the systems.

Barry Richmond, a pioneer in the field of systems thinking, described the concept of systems thinking as the "art and science of making reliable inferences about behavior, people, and systems by developing an increasingly deep understanding of the underlying structure and the fluid agents that interact to change the structure" (Richmond, 1994, pp. 2–3). Simply stated, key experts agree that systems thinking is the ability to embrace a holistic vision across the organization to see the crucial connections, interdependencies, and network of relationships among the moving agents.

Russell Ackoff is a famous systems thinking theorist who, during a keynote speaking event at Penn State University, used the analogy of understanding how a car works to explain systems thinking. In his analogy, he explains that if you were to take apart a car and lay out all the parts on the ground, you would have an engine, tires, pistons, a muffler, electronics, a frame, and so on, but you would no longer have a car (Ackoff, 2015). You would find it difficult to understand how to make the car run smoother or faster by examining any one of the individual parts. You can improve the car's function only when the machine is intact, with understanding of how all the pieces are interacting within the system(s).

There are different modes of inquiry that you can use to solve different types of problems. Analytical thinking is the science of dealing with an independent set of variables where the problem is dissected into parts and analyzed. Also called *reductionism*, analytical thinking centers on the belief that any problem can be explained by breaking down the problem into smaller parts. Analytical thinking is prevalent in organizations, as the focus is on solving the problem by dissecting the issue from a functional, product, or geographical point of view and by digging into the components or mechanisms that are causing the problem.

In contrast, systems thinking, also called *holism* or *synthesis*, is about understanding the whole rather than the parts and striving to understand the interacting elements and inner connections in a fluid state. Systems thinking is the best strategy for addressing ambiguity, as it is based on a worldview approach and develops your ability to understand and explore the dynamic systems at play, including how they interconnect and influence the whole.

Feedback loops, which are part of any system, can be either positive or negative; they are the clues elicited from the system's behavior. They show you that something is or is not going well. A positive feedback loop is a reinforcing relationship and is essentially what causes the same event again and again, whereas a negative feedback loop is a dynamic action that becomes weaker with iteration. Have you experienced a situation in which a decision created more issues over time, or caused the same problems to reoccur? Or maybe you've experienced an unpleasant surprise at work or at home because of a situation or someone's behavior? Feedback loops point to the behavior of the system and bring awareness of the changes within the system (some unexpected). They also help explain the unforeseen causes of events. By paying attention to the system's feedback loops, you can find evidence that may have led to the surprise, or, as stated by Ackoff (2015), the messy situation, and discover the issue's root cause.

Let's say an education administrator needs to examine their students' recent low math test scores (a feedback loop). An analytical or reductionist thinker might approach the program by interviewing each math teacher, researching the test questions, and reviewing the test scores before proposing a solution. A systems thinker would try to understand the teachers' experiences and teaching methods but also the outer sphere variables, such as the curriculum, school leadership, student demographics, funding, and many other elements. Systems thinking is about the moving parts, and it requires you to address the network of interrelated parts and how they influence one another and evolve along the way. Analytical thinking can teach us how something works, but systems thinking builds the broader base of informative action.

If you are tasked with helping the business become more efficient or more innovative or helping it create new growth channels, reviewing the business model, financial records, and corporate structure are all relevant. However, if you want to know how the business truly operates, you should learn more about how the executives and employees think, act, and make decisions within the processes and functions. The secret ingredient to understanding a business is to get into the invisible space, where the communication, thinking, and behavior patterns are located.

LEARNING INSIGHT

· · · · ·

Can you reflect on a time in the workplace when you should have applied systems thinking rather than analytical thinking to arrive at a more well-rounded solution?

COMPLEX ADAPTIVE SYSTEMS

The third main concept to understand regarding the ambiguity mindset is the complex adaptive system (CAS), which is defined by John Henry Holland, pioneer of complex adaptive systems research and professor of psychology and electrical engineering at the University of Michigan, as an "organization that has many components and as each component affects and is affected by, every other component within the boundaries of the systems such that one cannot appreciate the system's whole by simply examining the parts" (Holland, 2005, p. 1). Some complex adaptive systems include global companies, multinationals, and conglomerates that have fluid components, dynamic relationships, and interconnected systems. This also includes domains such as health care, military, and government agencies.

One of the interviewed executives from the education domain—Daniel—explained how his organization was a CAS, as it had a large number of elements that interacted in a nonlinear fashion. Daniel described how the UAE education system was taking a systems thinking approach to redefining education and schools as dynamic and adaptive, not rigid institutions. Daniel was part of the strategic reform plan to change the Arabic education curriculum into a CAS, whereby the revised curriculum reaches beyond the school walls into the social systems to create a new understanding of learning and development that includes input from corporate, government, and academic interests.

When working in CAS environments, you need to know that to operate, you must understand the changing decisions, information, and knowledge architecture within the systems, rather than try to fully control the system. What is interesting about working in a CAS is that to be successful, you need to be able to seek meaning from the fluid and dynamic system and view the organization as a living, changing organism.

Consider Carter, a manager who was continually on the edge of a frustrated outburst. Carter always focused on controlling all the data, processes, and outcomes. Whenever something happened that was unexpected, Carter became surprised, and his immediate reaction was an inflammatory outburst aimed at the team that usually included looking for someone to blame. Carter failed to understand that hierarchy control is not real control.

Even as an executive, you cannot control all workplace variables and all the changing behaviors of the employees. The internal systems are continually shifting; knowledge flows in and out of the organization, employees' motivations ebb and flow, and the external environment puts pressure on static processes. To thrive while working within a CAS, you will need to become comfortable with the unknown and learn to react with mindfulness and curiosity when faced with an outcome that is different from what you expected.

Many insightful strategies have ended up with unintended consequences, which are pervasive in a CAS. Sociologist Robert K. Merton coined the phrase "unintended consequences" when researching social change and described three types of unintended consequences: an unexpected benefit, which can be described as luck or serendipity; an unexpected drawback, or a detriment occurring in addition to the desired effect; and a perverse result, which is an aberrant effect contrary to what was originally intended (Merton, 1936, p. 894). Economists, scientists, and academics study unintended consequences to make better future decisions. Some examples include the following:

- Increasingly innovative vehicle airbags may cause an inadvertent behavior change; you may begin to drive more aggressively, as you feel safer, and thus are less safe overall.

- Despite the advancement of big data and the plethora of information at your fingertips, determining whether information is real or fake is difficult.

- International travel growth means you can travel anywhere in the world on any given day; however, this connectivity can and has caused rapid spread of viral diseases.

Think about the last time you experienced an unpleasant moment. Did you think the disruptive moment occurred out of the blue? More than likely, a series of smaller moments, or red flags, happened earlier. You normally don't pay attention to those small red flags, as the *causes* of the decisions are usually separated in time from when you experience the *effects*. When you don't pay attention to cause-effect events, you can't learn from your mistakes, as pinpointing the decision you made that created the larger, unintended consequence is hard. Essentially, your quest for rapid problem solving that improves the situation in the short term often creates larger problems in the long term, which propels more systemic problems.

A common example of short-term thinking is a company that may fire an employee at the first sign of poor performance. There is an assumption that fixing one part of the performance issue (the employee) will solve the problem; however, the corporate system is not defined by one person's lack of performance. Was it really the person's lack of performance that was affecting the company, or was it insufficient training, a lack of resources, or the corporate decision-making practices that caused the employee's poor performance?

There are also potential knock-on effects with high turnover (feedback loops), such as the company beginning to have a poor hiring reputation. Seeking future quality candidates may become difficult, there may be a loss of corporate knowledge, or other employees may begin to look for their own new job, as they worry they might be released next. You should also begin to think further than the original decision to begin anticipating any unintended consequences.

LEARNING INSIGHT

● ● ● ● ●

Think of a problematic situation that you experienced. In hindsight, what were some of the feedback loops that you should have paid attention to?

LEARNING FROM EXPERIENCE

The term *learning from experience* has been frequently used interchangeably with the concept of experiential learning. While the two concepts have many similarities, this book focuses on the former: the connection between learning from experience in informal situations and the nonroutine circumstances of the pursuit of learning ambiguity within the workplace (Marsick & Watkins, 1990).

David Kolb, former professor of organizational behavior at MIT Sloan School of Management and emeritus professor at Weatherhead School of Management, describes learning from experience as the "process whereby knowledge is created through the transformation of experience" (Kolb, 1984, p. 38). John Dewey, the philosopher of democracy and education, stated there are two essential components of learning from experience: the experience of the learner and critical inquiry (Dewey, 1938). Knowing this, to create an ambiguity mindset, you must be able to build your inquiry skills while you learn by doing, learn from others, learn through situations, learn through reflection, learn from community, and understand the importance of context and critical inquiry.

But it takes effort and time to reflect on an experience, because of the fast pace of decision-making in organizations, and you usually do not pay attention to the actual learning process to avoid future thinking or behavior errors. So how do you become motivated to learn from experience? And when dealing with ambiguity, how do you make sense of the experiences to make informed quality decisions?

In 1968, Malcolm Knowles, an educator who was focused on the science behind adult education, put forth a theory that distinguished adult learning (andragogy) from childhood learning (pedagogy). Andragogy theory approaches adult learning with the assumption that adults have their own set of life experiences and motivations, which enables them to learn better by doing, and they have their own desires and motivations to apply learning (Knowles, 1970). You need only to tell a manager who has been running a team for over ten years that they need to attend a mandatory leadership course to see their motivation fizzle and their eyes glaze over. If you were to dig into the manager's learning motivation, you may find that the manager would like to learn more about team dynamics or conflict resolution rather than having to focus on leadership fundamentals.

Consider Santiago, a manager who in an executive coaching session spoke excitedly about his latest personal passion project. Essentially, he was building an extension to his house's deck and informed the coach of the dozens of weekend hours he spent watching YouTube videos to learn more about deck building. While learning how to build a deck was obviously not a requirement for the job, Santiago's motivation was to learn what was relevant and interesting to him, in this case, revisiting old calculus formulas to verify wood cutting measurements. Have you ever wondered why you were motivated to learn more about a certain topic or to explore different experiences than some of your colleagues or friends? There is an underlying relationship between the cognitive, emotional, and attitudinal elements of adult learning.

Learning how adults like to learn is important. It is now widely accepted among adult learning experts that there are at least seven different adult learning principles (Knowles, 1970):

- As adults mature, they increasingly move toward self-directed learning and want to be in charge of their learning journey.

- Adults use their life experiences to facilitate learning and "learn by doing."

- Adults prefer to know how the information is relevant and find most relevance from learning that aligns with their social, life, or own realities.

- Adult learning is problem-centered; adults want to apply the new learning immediately.

- Adults are motivated by internal rather than external factors and will learn when they feel they need to learn something.

- Adults want information that helps them improve their situation and prefer to choose their learning options (and not be told what to learn).

- Adults learn best in informal situations and with real-world problems.

Knowing the adult learning principles, Dr. Pamela Booth Rosati conducted research using behavior analysis to understand how midlevel corporate leaders could become more insightful and deliberate communicators and learn how to manage the interpersonal and communication nuances of senior leadership roles. A global pharma company commissioned Rosati and her team to create a sustained corporate behavioral change. At the start of the leadership program, Rosati and her team categorized the participants' actions as exhibiting initiating behaviors (proposing and building ideas), reacting behaviors (supporting, disagreeing, defending, and attacking), clarifying behaviors (seeking or giving information, testing understanding, seeking reasons, and summarizing), or process behaviors (shutting down others, bringing others in, and labeling their behaviors for others) in an effort to verify how some participants used those tactics during group discussions.

Over a few days, the participants discussed tough corporate scenarios to debate and agree on during the roundtable discussions. The behavior analysis facilitators recorded the number and type of behaviors observed in each of the participants, focusing on what kind of statement each person said from a category perspective versus what they said from a content perspective (Booth, 2019).

Even though the participants knew they were being observed, they frequently resorted to default communication behaviors to get their way or prove their point in the sometimes-heated discussions. After the sessions, the facilitator met with the participants in groups and in one-on-one discussions to review the summary of observed behaviors in concert with feedback from their peers. Only during the critical reflection period did the participants recognize their default communication behaviors. Once they were able to see in quantitative numbers and percentages how much of their time they spent advocating for their own views, rather than inquiring about the views of others, and when that matched up with the feedback given by their peers in the exercise, they began to understand their thinking and behavior patterns and adjust to create better leadership outcomes. Learning from past experiences is often a precursor to transforming future experiences with better results.

You should avoid making repeated mistakes in routine situations, but when you're immersed in new situations, mistakes are common and should be embraced as learning opportunities. Think back to Carter, who was always on the verge of a frustrated outburst. To learn from the experience (the error), Carter shouldn't have yelled at the team but could have used appreciative inquiry to ask, "What was happening when the error occurred? Why did the error happen? How can we implement better thinking and behavior mechanisms to avoid future errors?"

LEARNING INSIGHT

· · · · ·

Identify a negative experience that recently occurred. Reflect on two or three things that should be learned and incorporated into future decisions.

Key Takeaways

Systems thinking is a misunderstood strategic method of inquiry. You should grasp the fact that systems thinking is not about technical or mechanical systems and is more about becoming aware of the various interactions and interrelationships within a fluid and dynamic environment; it's about being able to see the whole rather than the parts.

Feedback loops are an input from within the system. When immersed in a complex adaptive system or uncertain situations, you must pay attention to both positive and negative feedback loops to identify the issue that is at the root. While feedback loops are inherently difficult to understand, you should start paying attention to the changes of the systems you are in and try to understand the source of workplace surprises, recurring errors, or unexpected outcomes.

Use a mental model with a wide-angle lens. Just knowing your technical job is not enough. You must have an open mind and embrace an open system in which the people, the job, and the elements are continually changing. Embrace different perspectives and multiple realities so you can make better decisions. We all interpret information differently, come from different backgrounds, and have different viewpoints on how to accomplish a process. Teams with diverse views are able to create more well-rounded solutions.

Learn from your experiences. Reflecting on past experiences to seek meaning and to learn from them is essential for personal and professional growth.

Develop an ambiguity mindset. To build an ambiguity mindset, you must be able to build the cognitive and behavior capacity to reflect on, examine, and adapt perspectives and to seek meaning from dynamic connections, interactions, experiences, and behaviors to determine the ideal decision pathway.

A Starting Point

As we begin to explore the five ambiguity thinking and behavior strategies, I would like to provide a tool to enable you to seek deeper understanding of your current ambiguity mindset: a self-assessment questionnaire.

This questionnaire is the starting point. The self-assessment is your personal measurement gauge, needed first and foremost, because the ability to understand ambiguity is still difficult to measure or even observe. You will be the judge to verify whether your thinking and behavior patterns have changed over time.

You should take the self-assessment, which follows this chapter, now and then do it again when you finish the book (see Appendix A). I encourage you to take five minutes to measure your comfort level—the baseline behavior and thinking level when you are confronted with paradoxes or confusing or ill-defined problems. You can compare the results once you reach the end of the book.

Alternatively, you can review the original Intolerance of Ambiguity assessment, which was created by Stanley Budner in 1962.

Dealing with Ambiguity: Self-Assessment Questionnaire

Place an "X" in the number space that relates best to your current comfort level for each question with the following scale: 1, very uncomfortable; 2, somewhat uncomfortable; 3, comfortable; 4, somewhat comfortable; 5, very comfortable. The questions relate to the three decoding principles.

RATE YOUR COMFORT LEVEL FOR THE FOLLOWING AREAS:	1	2	3	4	5
To acknowledge that "not knowing" is okay during unexpected situations					
To embrace inexactness, paradoxes, or uncertain situations					
To take the time needed to understand the potential consequences of faulty perspective taking					
To compare own perspective with diverse or alternative views to verify differences					
To explore the different behaviors in the workplace or the systems you are in					
To resist making quick decisions and delay providing a response					
To adapt project direction with unstructured or unclear schedules or targets					
To be curious in knowledge gap situations					
To seek to work or live in uncertain, chaotic, or unstructured environments					
To find different social networks to find conflicting or paradoxical information					
To adopt new attitudes or behaviors from different cultural beliefs					
To be prepared to learn new things when faced with unfamiliar situations					

CHAPTER 1

. . . . .

CREATE POWERFUL INSIGHTS THROUGH CRITICAL REFLECTION

The first thinking and behavior strategy is the concept of critical reflection. In fact, all the executives I interviewed for this book exhibited reflective thinking and practices as part of their mental models (their beliefs, perceptions, and principles) that assisted them through unfamiliar challenges. The adult development and learning theorist Jack Mezirow defined *critical reflection* as the "ability to unearth, examine, and change deeply held or fundamental assumptions" (Mezirow, 1991). Essentially, to conduct critical reflection, you must apply a concerted effort to challenge your own assumptions and routine ways of thinking to form a new behavior or action. The act of critical reflection is not merely a look backward at past events to pave the way forward with a different decision; rather, you need to integrate a full situational understanding of the past to create a new learned behavior and action. The ambiguity mindset goal is to determine that, while being an expert in your field is a professional achievement, you need to uncover the hidden beliefs that keep you in a limiting comfort zone.

Atul Gawande wrote the article "Personal Best" in 2011 for *The New Yorker* about his experience working as a surgeon and seeking performance coaching advice. Atul was mindful of his successful surgeries over the previous eight years, as he tracked his results with the national database and consistently beat the averages. In recent years, however, Atul had noticed that his rate of quality care, a measurement of medical issues, was no longer going down, as it should. He wondered whether he had reached his professional peak.

Atul noted that sports athletes, musicians, and actors used performance coaches, and even executives are now comfortable using executive coaches. He wondered why doctors did not use them. He knew that seeking guidance was a risky move. The general perception was that, once you become a doctor, you are the master of your craft, and having a performance coach might be seen as a weakness or lack of expertise. Atul was aware that he might receive harsh judgment from his peers, which could affect his career. But he considered the alternatives and decided to contact an esteemed retired general surgeon, Dr. Osteen. Atul had worked under him during Atul's residency training. Dr. Osteen agreed to watch Atul's surgeries and provide feedback.

The retired general surgeon attended one of Atul's surgeries, and while he watched silently throughout the entire procedure, he provided small but insightful comments in the doctors' lounge afterward. Dr. Osteen had noticed that Atul had positioned the patient perfectly in front of Atul but not in a position that suited the other surgical attendees. This resulted in the surgical draping being askew for the surgical assistant across the table, on the patient's right side; this restricted the surgical attendee's left arm and hampered his ability to fully see the surgical wound.

At one point, the surgical team found themselves struggling to see high enough into the surgical area. The draping also pushed the medical student off to the surgical assistant's right, where he couldn't help at all. Additionally, Atul should have made more room to the left side, which would have allowed the surgical assistant to hold the retractor and free the surgical assistant's left hand. Further feedback included that Atul's elbows periodically rose to the level of his shoulders, which means less precision and unnecessary fatigue.

Finally, Dr. Osteen observed that Atul was wearing magnifying loupes to ensure a laser focus on the patient, but Atul did not seem to be aware of how much of his peripheral vision was affected. This resulted in Atul's inability to monitor the anesthesiologist or how the operating light had drifted away from the surgical area.

It is a humbling experience to be an expert in your field and be open and honest enough to invite performance feedback into your practice, but Atul described the experience as enlightening and stated, "That one twenty-minute discussion with Dr. Osteen gave me more to consider and work on than I'd had in the past five years" (Gawande, 2011). By challenging your own and other people's assumptions through a variety of mechanisms, you can reach outside of your own "I am an expert" mindset. By channeling critical reflection, you must challenge yourself by asking probing questions of your past experiences and thinking patterns to provide a better cognitive framework when faced with hidden barriers or uncertainty in the future.

HIDDEN BARRIERS

Not surprisingly, the concept of critical reflection creates paradoxical tensions, as many fast-paced companies are programmed to keep moving forward and to disregard past events, bulldoze through perceived barriers, or disregard recurring issues to meet the annual or quarterly targets. Interestingly, various cognitive mechanisms work against you that create potential barriers to conducting accurate critical reflection, such as the Ebbinghaus's forgetting curve, which indicates that the speed of forgetting will increase when you endure physiological factors such as stress and lack of sleep (Loftus, 1985). Trusting your memory may not be the best mechanism when you are faced with stressful ambiguous situations.

Neuroscience may also be against you. Research shows that your brain is biased; you may unconsciously downplay past painful experiences or blur them from your memory to protect your self-confidence. Your memory of good experiences may also be flawed, as you tend to see your past good moments as more impressive than the events actually were. And finally, in your recollection of the past event, you may fail to recall additional external elements or may lack a full 360° review of the situation.

Even if you are absolutely sure of your expertise as a seasoned executive with years of successful progression in your career, research supports the need for critical reflection. For example, the overconfidence bias is the tendency to overestimate your abilities and talent. A 2018 article in *PLOS* journal included a study in which 2,821 participants were asked to rate the statement "I am more intelligent than the average person," and the results (in part) showed that 65 percent of participants believed they were smarter than average, with more men likely to agree than women (Heck et al., 2018). Additionally, Dr. Tasha Eurich, an organizational psychologist and principal of the Eurich Group, conducted a research study with more than 3,600 leaders across a variety of roles and industries and found that, relative to lower-level leaders, higher-level leaders more significantly overvalued their skills (compared with others' perceptions) (Eurich, 2018). One of the research explanations is that high-level leaders simply have fewer people giving them candid feedback.

Similarly, David Dunning and Justin Kruger, social psychologists from Cornell University, developed the concept of the *Dunning-Kruger effect*, which is a type of cognitive bias that causes people to overestimate their knowledge or ability, particularly in areas where they have little to no experience. This may be a valid concept to remember when working in uncertainty and ambiguous situations. The Dunning-Kruger effect suggests that, when you don't know something, you aren't aware of your own lack of knowledge and may exaggerate your competence. In other words, you don't know what you don't know, and you don't even know it.

A DELIBERATE PAUSE

To avoid the double burden of a lack of awareness and a lack of experience with uncertainty, the act of critical reflection allows you to take a deliberate pause and helps you think through messy situations. Taking a deliberate pause is crucial for your own self-development; it gives you time to reflect, to seek feedback, to consider alternative views, and to uncover hidden assumptions. Embracing critical reflection to generate new insights leads to becoming better at articulating questions, confronting bias, and examining cause-effect situations.

Adult learning theorists are continuing to explore the ways in which reflective practice can increase understanding, expand one's perspective, and improve learning outcomes. David Kolb, a psychologist and educational theorist, developed a four-stage cycle of learning that incorporates the reflective process as a fundamental component (Kolb, 1984). Kolb's model is widely used in leadership and education programs and is a key source for understanding how adults learn through discovery and experience.

David Kolb's experiential learning cycle also provides a useful way to describe how you may gravitate toward a specific way of learning, but more importantly, it can provide a process for a continuum of learning through experience. As illustrated by Lauren Wolfsfeld and Muhammad M. Haj-Yahia in "Learning and Supervisory Styles in the Training of Social Workers," Kolb's continuous learning process includes four parts: concrete experience, reflective observation, abstract conceptualization, and active experimentation (see Figure 3).

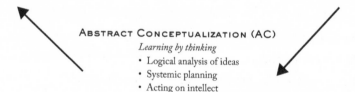

CONCRETE EXPERIENCE (CE)
Learning by experiencing
• Learn from specific experience
• Relate to people
• Be sensitive to people's feelings

ACTIVE EXPERIMENTATION (AE)
Learning by doing
• Get things done
• Take risks
• Influence people/events
  through actions

REFLECTIVE OBSERVATION (RO)
Learning by reflecting
• Careful observation
• Diverse perspectives
• Search for meaning

ABSTRACT CONCEPTUALIZATION (AC)
Learning by thinking
• Logical analysis of ideas
• Systemic planning
• Acting on intellect

FIGURE 3. KOLB'S LEARNING CYCLE
(SOURCE: WOLFSFELD AND HAJ-YAHIA, 2010, P. 71)

Dr. Aamir A. Rehman is a partner in an investment firm and conducted a qualitative research study with fifteen private equity professionals who worked in high-stakes environments, in which decisions can result in millions of dollars in gains or losses for the firm. The purpose of the research was to learn how the private equity professionals described the role of learning from experience in their work. He wanted to determine what specific learning behavior strategies they'd report using, and to learn how the business model or other organizational factors of private equity supported or hindered learning from experience. Rehman found that, placing the private equity internal investment four-step model as an overlay onto the Kolb learning cycle model, there were similarities in how private equity professionals analyzed their clients' investments (Rehman, 2020).

One of the research findings revealed that, when the participants were asked to think of an example of a time when they learned from an experience at work, 66 percent of them identified an investment disappointment, while 33 percent cited a complex transition as a key experiential learning event (Rehman, 2020).

These results aligned with all four of Kolb's stages. The first stage, concrete experience, was shown in their daily work in the office. The second stage, reflecting on experience, was shown in the ways the participants discussed their investments after the fact with contacts, and sometimes even wrote about them. The participants also reported that they conceptualized the lessons from their investments that aligned with the third stage of Kolb's model, abstract conceptualization. Finally, the participants stated they had applied the learning-from-experience lessons to subsequent investments, which mirrors the model's fourth stage, active experimentation.

This tool can be useful to assess your own learning from experience. Be sure to verify that you have moved through all steps in the cycle rather than just getting stuck in the first phase (concrete experiences). Kolb suggested that failure to complete the learning cycle can lead to a failure to assimilate your learning from the experience, resulting in the repetition of poor strategies or in assumption-based solutions.

THINKING PRACTICES

Many executives have already learned the value of conducting critical reflection to assess their past thinking patterns and actions. During the interviews, the executives discussed past events and provided insights on how they were able to derive meaning from complex experiences to learn how to understand ambiguous situations with better clarity.

CREATE MEANING

The executives I interviewed had the cognitive ability (the confidence and independence) to create meaning from their actions and were then able to construct knowledge from the event, to transfer the knowledge to new situations, and to seek meaning from the new situation in order to understand the previous ambiguous situation. It sounds simple and logical, but self-reflection is one of the top leadership competencies, and leadership courses are a multibillion-dollar enterprise for a reason. Not many people take the time to review their past experiences and understand them, much less assess their thinking patterns or insights and subsequently make changes to their behavior.

Here are some of the narratives from the executives I interviewed for this book as they discussed their reflective mental models, beliefs, and thinking principles while working in uncertain situations. Charlie, the renewable energy executive, stated that "everything was very ambiguous, and since I was so embedded in the world, I just assumed that I'm creating my own universe. If you have that approach to life and to your work, then of course you get very intimate with the activity and what's going on." It is important to understand that your worldview can keep expanding, and as you gain insights, your perspectives will also change.

Supporting the cognitive ability to seek meaning to help explore your assumptions, the information and technology executive—Karim—said the following when discussing a complex and unique hypothetical question with his counterparts: "I asked the two presenters a question, and it was evident that they didn't have a readily available answer. One of them was already leaning toward an 'it depends' type of answer, until the second presenter had the guts to say, 'I don't know,' and he earned my respect right there. I value this simplicity and directness." It may be frustrating as an executive to not have or give a definitive answer in all situations, but you need to realize that a linear thinking answer to a complex issue will only give you comfort that the decision was made, and it may not provide the best decision.

Systems can be understood by looking for patterns that could describe a potential evolution of that system. To that point, Rachid, the oil and gas executive I interviewed for the book, was in a unique and strategic position within this industry; he interacted with all the oil and gas players on a global stage at both the government and corporate levels. Rachid was tasked with pursuing an energy program that provided a sustainable and profitable remit while strengthening and growing upstream exploration and the production sector. Rachid created meaning when faced with a puzzling pattern of events related to ambiguity and stated, "You have principles, you know. You have hindsight—a perspective. If there are no precedents, if you try hard enough, you will find that even if you set your imagination on whatever information you have available, you can compile imaginary precedents to provide context for the situation."

When faced with a unique set of challenges, your memory reflects on all your learned experiences to verify whether there is a similar past situation or patterns that may help pinpoint a direction.

KNOW THYSELF

Why is the concept of self-awareness during times of uncertainty so critical? You see executives all the time talking about corporate values—teamwork, collaboration, or integrity—but you often notice that the executive's actions are not aligned with these values. This misalignment can cause fissures in effective leadership.

The theorists Chris Argyris, professor emeritus at Harvard Business School, and Donald Schön, professor in urban planning at MIT, conducted research on workplace behavior and wrote about the ideal self and actual selves. They asserted that people hold maps in their heads about how to plan, implement, and review their actions, but few people are aware that those maps do not necessarily match up with the theories the person explicitly espouses (Argyris & Schön, 1974). This means that some executives, either consciously or unconsciously, don't act according to their own ideologies.

The Johari window communication model, created in 1955 by Joseph Luft and Harry Ingham, is a conceptual box divided into four quadrants and is a psychological tool to help you understand your relationship with yourself and with others (see Figure 4). The horizontal axis of the window represents your knowledge of yourself (whether information is known or unknown to you), and the vertical axis is others' knowledge about your communication intent (known or unknown to them). For example, you may not realize that you have a tendency to interrupt people when they're speaking and that it's causing frustration within the team; this information is unknown to you. But you may think that, since you are the manager, your team expects and even wants you to talk more. This is an example of the blind quadrant, known by others but unknown by self.

In the blind quadrant, you may not be aware of certain aspects of your own personality, but other people can see and feel them. In the hidden quadrant—known to self, unknown to others—you may have certain fears or insecurities, and you may try to hide those vulnerable traits

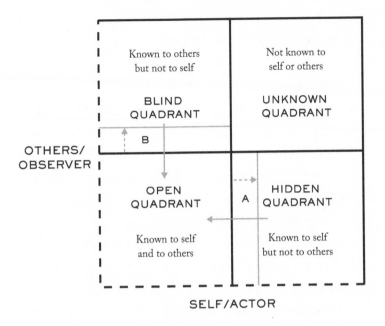

FIGURE 4. THE JOHARI WINDOW
(SOURCE: BOXER, PERREN, AND BERRY, 2013, P. 60)

from the people around you. Over time, these insecurities can sap your energy as you try to avoid certain situations. The unknown quadrant—unknown to self, unknown to others—is part of your self-discovery and potential. Through discussion, you can learn more about your own behaviors and thinking limitations and create new learning experiences.

The goal of the Johari window is to test out your assumptions through dialogue and help you move into the open quadrant, the known knowns, where you are able to show yourself and be known by others. This self-awareness and outward authenticity builds trust and confidence in those around you.

LEADERSHIP MIRROR

I received my first 360° review while leading an airline training academy. The point of a 360° review is to seek feedback from all around you—not just from your managers but also from your direct reports, peers, customers, and other stakeholders. I remember assisting in the creation of the thirty leadership questions. I even remember commenting that we should have positive and negative comment boxes for each leadership competency, thinking that providing space for additional comments would be beneficial. I also remember being comfortable with the idea of having my manager and my sixteen-member training team give me feedback because I thought we were a highly functioning team.

Weeks later, I was asked to meet with my manager, and she gave me a large yellow envelope about three inches thick and said, "Read these assessments, and let me know your plan of action." I didn't understand how the survey could generate so much data, but when I got home and started reading the comments, I realized the survey had been sent to the training team, as well as to the 1,200 flight attendants. And every negative comment box had a comment. I quickly read the top three pages, and I saw that many of the comments were aimed directly at me. The other comments were . . . well, just negative. I was mortified.

After I picked myself up off the floor and put aside my ego, I reread all the comments and noticed that the majority of the comments had three main themes: The flight attendants were frustrated with a lack of head office support, a lack of corporate information, and a feeling of abandonment when issues arose during flights and at the outstations.

I realized through critical reflection that we had a lot of work to do to address these issues, and I also needed to consider how I might have contributed to their frustration. Through discussion with the senior team and analysis of everyone's recommendations, the department created various mechanisms for the flight attendants to feel secure, informed, and supported while flying and while staying at outstations. This included better internal communication channels, a help line for sensitive and confidential issues, and better training processes for both the pilots and the flight attendants to ensure a cohesive team during all scheduled rotations.

Perturbation is when you are jolted with surprising information that makes you pause and reflect. Before you get slammed with a perturbation, learn how to take a periodic deliberate pause to verify how your behavior is affecting others during times of uncertainty to avoid larger issues that may simmer and erupt later.

CHALLENGING ASSUMPTIONS

The various emotional intelligence, leadership, numeric, and verbal reasoning assessments in a 360° review are all very powerful tools for becoming more self-aware in order to leverage operational efficiencies. In the book *Multipliers*, Liz Wiseman and Greg McKeown delineate two groups of managers: those who multiply the talent of those around them and those who diminish it (Wiseman & McKeown, 2010).

Consider this quick leadership exercise: A facilitator would ask the participants to use a sticky note to list the qualities of a manager who multiplies the talents of others. Dozens of colorful sticky notes fill the wall, with phrases such as "believes in my talent," "trusts and motivates me," and "gives me challenging work," and a list of positive manager attributes is generated. The next step is to list the diminishing traits. Most of the sticky note comments are "micromanages," "takes credit for my deliverables," "never gives feedback," "does not let me talk in meetings," and so on. The list is very large (Wiseman & McKeown, 2010).

Next, the participants/managers in the room recognize themselves as diminishers—or at least realize they embody some of those traits. They must challenge their assumptions of why and how they conduct these diminisher actions in the name of good business management. The managers must acknowledge how they thought exhibiting power and authority over a team was good for building high-performance teams. They must acknowledge that they had potentially been inhibiting the team they were supposed to be supporting, guiding, and developing.

Dr. Renee Owen, assistant professor at Southern Oregon University, conducted adult learning research to discover the lived experiences of teachers who employ secular spiritual pedagogical practices and to learn more about what spirituality looks and feels like in the classrooms and how the teachers reflect on how they make meaning of their experiences (Owen, 2019).

Teaching is a high-stress and emotional job that presents daily *disorienting dilemmas*. Jack Mezirow, an adult learning theorist, defined *disorienting dilemma* as a perspective transformation that occurs when an unexpected incident challenges your expectations and worldview (Mezirow, 1991). During Owen's research interviews, the teachers told stories about their struggles and failures as teachers and how openness and reflection helped them learn through the pain of those experiences. One of the teachers told a story about receiving a crushing negative review from a student and how the teacher had to reconcile his defensive reaction and ego with his higher self. Owen states that teachers use reflection techniques to examine their lives and self-reflect on their mistakes, something they have to do without being defensive or they wouldn't be able to model the equanimity and compassion they teach their students to have (Owen, 2019).

Similarly, the executives I interviewed were highly regarded experts in their domains and had years of progressive successful achievements; however, they still described inner reflective moments (some painful) that spoke to their ability to self-analyze and decode their mental models with stunning humbleness and honest thoughtfulness, and they took action from the reflection. The executives reflected on the interview question "Tell me how your beliefs and perceptions of ambiguity may have influenced how your ambiguity mindset was formed."

Charlie, the renewable energy executive, responded, "I've had the opportunity to think about that question because I was wondering why I could manage these multicultural environments and the bit of chaos navigation. It has to do with my childhood, actually. It turns out that having no dad and living in a ghetto is a real good teaching experience. Realizing that crisis is a part of every day, that, in the worst situation, almost nobody will agree with your point of view, and then maturing to the fact that there's a reason for that and then learning how to deal with that is crucial." To that point, your belief system regarding ambiguity may have been formed long before you entered the workplace.

In response to disturbing moments, in which the conscious mind is forced to notice contradictions, the executives learned how to become more humble and self-reflective during their career progression. One of the executives stated that he thought career progression was based on knowledge and technical abilities but slowly discovered that there were many factors beyond that simplistic view: "Your basic expertise gets you to a certain level, and then you realize that you actually don't know that much and that there's a lot you haven't tapped into."

Your beliefs and attitudes are developed from childhood and may have contributed to your limitations dealing with ambiguity or, quite the opposite, helped you become more comfortable in unstable environments. Your childhood experiences may provide clues to your current ambiguity thinking and behavior patterns.

LEARNING INSIGHT

· · · · ·

Can you think of any perturbing moments or critical events that occurred in your past that may have helped form your beliefs, values, or perceptions regarding ambiguity?

ARE YOU THE SUBJECT OR THE OBJECT?

You could assume, because you are an adult with a university degree and a certain level of expertise and are a contributing member of society, that you have a high cognitive maturity level. In fact, you may not have learned how to push yourself to make meaning of differing worldviews or to stretch your ability to learn when immersed in your surroundings. Harvard professor Robert Kegan introduced his subject-object theory in his book *In Over Our Heads* (1994), which focuses on how an individual acquires knowledge, constructs definitions of their own worldviews, and makes meaning from either a subject or object perspective.

In this case, *subject* refers to things that you identify with or fixate on or an assumption about how the world works. In essence, the things you can't see but that are a part of you. On the other hand, *object* refers to things that you can reflect on, take control of, or be responsible for. Object is a more complex worldview, as you can see *and* act on things (Kegan, 1994). When you are immersed in a troublesome ambiguous situation, you may tend to focus on self and your assumptions within the confusion as your mind tries to fill in the blanks from missing information. However, by shifting to the more holistic object view, you are able to increase your capacity to take on additional perspectives and be able to see the different shades of gray instead of only black or white, moving away from only right or wrong viewpoints.

Think back to the last time you lost your cool with a colleague or friend. When you reflect on the event, were you the subject of the issue, with all your emotions and feelings immersed in the dilemma? Or were you able to detach yourself from the issue and clearly see the issue from a different perspective? Were you able to keep your emotions and frustration in check? Kegan claims that you should strive to move from being a subject toward being an object, essentially building your ability to think and develop within more complex social systems and learning to make sense of the increasingly complex world (Kegan, 1994).

LEARNING INSIGHT

· · · · ·

If you find yourself in an emotional loop and feel as if you are the center of the issue, try to take an omnipresent view of all the different people's viewpoints. The emotional element will be removed, and you will begin to have more clarity.

To help understand the subject-object concept, recall Carter, who frequently berates his team in meetings with verbiage such as "I have wasted my time on this problem long enough. I don't understand why you all can't complete the project." Carter is stuck in the *I* mode, and everything revolves around his point of view; he's stuck in the subject role. Even highly educated executives may be stuck in this lower level of thinking, which means they tend to make decisions based on their own perceptions rather than more collaborative insights.

Or consider a group of marketing managers who continually debate the best course of action when a project is delayed. One of the managers is continually frustrated that his point of view is not being considered while in these high-pressure, fast-paced meetings. He thinks that the other managers are marginalizing him. When the manager received coaching on how to move from the subject to the object state of mind, he began to see his own emotional state when he was stuck in subject mode. By becoming more the object of the situation, he began to see the different points of view without any emotional attachment. Over time, he became less frustrated during the meetings and was able to contribute more effectively.

BEHAVIORAL PRACTICES

Not only were the executives I interviewed conducting critical reflection, a thinking exercise, but also they were doing some sort of action, a behavioral practice, as part of their professional routine to understand uncertain and ambiguous situations.

This was evident when Marcus, the shipping executive, was describing a difficult board meeting in which the board members did not seem to understand or accept a proposal. Marcus believed his proposal was comprehensive and logical, and provided the board members with enough information and context to deliver a swift approval. However, Marcus noted the diversity and cultural differences of the board members and wondered whether his manner of presenting was the most effective approach. He quickly changed the narrative to focus on new perspectives but noted with quick reflection his feeling of frustration and described a coping mechanism: "I guess [during those moments], you run up your personal hill to the top and scream and then let the dust settle. I try to reflect it back. . . . I try to find out the frustration and reflect on that and move to a new tactic." When Marcus quickly changed the intent of the message and reframed his mindset to target a more personalized pitch rather than focusing on the corporate requirements, the board members softened and became more interested in the proposal.

REFLECTION IN ACTION

Theorist Donald Schön calls this midstream shift in direction *reflection in action*, which he contrasts with *reflection on action* or looking at the situation *after* it is complete (Schön, 1983). The premise is that, with reflection in action, Marcus was learning in the moment that the original strategy was not working and proceeded to pivot to a revised strategy: reflection in the moment + instant learning = new action.

Karim, our information and technology executive, likes to use analogies when discussing past experiences to help formulate an understanding of a unique problem. He described this cognitive ability by describing the act of downhill skiing to visualize a solution to a fast-moving corporate dilemma. As Karim stated, "When you race in alpine skiing, you visualize every turn. You need to see yourself going through every turn and assess how you've performed so far, and what you need to do in order to prepare and adapt for the next turns. One of the things that was very important for me as a racer was to learn how to visualize the entire race. Each race is comprised of around sixty turns, and each turn is an opportunity to excel or to fail. You are constantly adapting your approach." Over time, you will become proficient at reflection in action and will be able to pivot to better thinking and decision options when faced with multiple decision pathways.

Certain domains are proficient in implementing critical reflection mechanisms; health care and nursing programs are domains highly recognized for putting theory into action. Amy, the health care executive, explained, "Every morning is a safety hub. Everyone, all the chief executives, all the managers and quality people, we get into a room and ask, 'What happened in the last twenty-four hours? Were there any special events that occurred?' Then [anyone] can say what's on their mind to share. This type of activity didn't present itself as a best practice until the last five years." Amy described how the safety huddle practice promotes a blameless culture by ensuring that speaking up about mistakes is encouraged. She also cited the best practice to create a corporate culture whereby if an employee hides an error and the error is later discovered, the employee may lose their job.

Other executives provided narratives that pointed toward after-action reviews as corporate learning and reflection mechanisms. However, in certain corporate cultures, after-action reviews are still seen as painful events, as many executives have a difficult time admitting that problems occurred during a project. Interestingly, Hazel, our entrepreneurial executive, was energetic when discussing strategies on how to manage difficult projects and was supportive of after-action reviews with the team. She said with a smile, "I'm always massively curious to figure out why we did what we did." I love this statement. By adopting this mantra, you can avoid the default negative thinking pattern that is to find fault or blame.

The reflective practice asks you to think about the behavior as it happens. The executives I interviewed instinctively recognized the changing dynamics of a situation before they took action. For example, the renewable energy executive, Charlie, described a cognitive thinking process involved in noticing paradoxes. "It's a really interesting paradox, in fact, where the partners are going faster than the corporate governance. That doesn't happen too often. You have a sense of urgency in the middle of that. Using my experience, I've realized something else gets unlocked in my head and presents a better solution." The executives' thinking and behavior architecture was to reflect, both in and on action, to retrieve information from memory, and then transfer the knowledge gained into new action or insight.

REFLECTIVE JOURNALING

Another practice that can help you learn from nonproductive thinking patterns is reflective journaling. Journaling can capture changes in perception and can increase your ability to analyze difficult situations. Educators have long known the benefits of journaling in the classroom;

students learn to journal by describing an event, their feelings, and their beliefs and write down any learning insights to increase their problem-solving strategies. Therapists advocate for their clients to use journaling as a tool to improve their clients' mental models, to resolve inner and external conflicts, and to create alignment with their spiritual, emotional, and physical health. And academics also use journaling to keep track of research ideas, to track resources, and to describe theoretical insights.

Journaling as a business tool is less prevalent, but academic practitioners are seeking ways to integrate this valuable learning activity into the corporate environment. The intent is to help develop cognitive pattern pathways that ultimately help manage fast-paced environments and allow you to reflect on how you think and act.

Reflective journaling is not simply the act of writing stream-of-consciousness thoughts. It is an introspective act that can change your surface awareness and help you examine your perceptions, thinking, feelings, and actions. Executives may not be using diaries, but they are using their day planners, phone apps, and online tools to record their thoughts. Many executive coaches and facilitators at academic executive courses at Columbia, INSEAD, Harvard, and other esteemed executive leadership centers such as Center for Creative Leadership (CCL) also promote the use of self-reflective journaling.

I was involved in a course project with Dr. Lisa Brooks and Dr. Monique Dawkins at Columbia University in which eighteen professional women were asked to journal for fourteen days to verify whether journaling enabled them to question their assumptions and change their behavior through action, essentially allowing them to synthesize different perspectives (whether from other people or simply new ideas) (Brooks et al., 2017). The participants could use a provided journal or their own resources, such as apps or notebooks, for their private journal entries. They were provided with eleven different journal prompts, such as "What behaviors did I display today?," "What emotions was I feeling?," and "What did I learn today about myself?" After the fourteen days, the participants completed a survey to indicate whether the reflective journaling exercise had been beneficial in helping them question their assumptions. A majority of the journal writers (82 percent) agreed with two of the survey items: "I believe that taking the time and effort to conduct reflective journaling can be a good business practice" and "I believe that I have gained personal knowledge or insights from the reflective journaling experience."

These highly accomplished women found value in the exercise. A few of them admitted that their journal entries during the first few days were somewhat task oriented and were about what they did that day. However, as the days went on, they began to notice patterns in their behaviors that may have contributed to various thinking and behavior habits. One participant stated, "I realize that I may be too driven; I usually feel unproductive if my day is not packed with deliverables, meetings, or activities. One of my insights was that I began to understand my own drive or nervous energy and how it affected others. I need to find a better way to channel this energy instead of making everyone crazy around me!" Other comments included, "I recognized that I had not been taking the time to reflect on my day's events. It almost is like I am robotic with the daily goings on in my life." Another participant came away with some interesting positive thinking and behavior pattern insights: "I realized that I am more effective in both my personal life and professional life than I often give myself credit for being. After a few days of journaling, I realized that I am doing a good job at being a mother, lawyer, wife, and activist" (Brooks et al., 2017).

The results of journaling can be life changing or can contribute to minor life shifts. Either way, through the practice of reflection, you will develop a deeper appreciation for understanding not only your own thinking patterns but also other people's situations and how they think, learn, and show up at work.

Take your own deliberate pause. Find a hard-copy journal that you will keep with you for the next few weeks or an online tool that you can keep confidential. Write down insights of any problematic, confusing projects or uncertain situations that you may be experiencing. Keep a few questions in mind to ensure you are not just writing your grocery list or a to-do list, such as:

- What sort of strong behaviors did I exhibit and in what context during the uncertain situation?

- What were my emotional triggers when I was immersed in the confusion?

- What assumptions did I hold regarding the difficult situation?

If you find yourself getting irritated at something or someone during the workplace difficult moments, write down what is happening in that moment, such as who or what you are irritated at and what the emotional trigger was.

Remember that critical reflection helps expand your viewpoint and decision-making capability, acknowledge alternative beliefs, and create a bridge between information and wisdom. I have included some journal prompts in Appendix B that may be helpful. Pick one of the prompts and track your daily thoughts on the situations you experienced. Feel free to ramble, draw pictures, or tell a story. I suspect that, after a week or so, you will begin to see a consistent behavior and thinking pattern, and therein is the value. This is not an exercise or habit you need to do for your entire life, just for a short period of time, for a few weeks, so you can start to see patterns in your thinking, behavior, and emotional triggers.

Key Takeaways

Take a deliberate pause. Taking a deliberate pause to reflect on difficult and uncertain situations that occurred is important to capture hidden insights. Ask yourself at least three questions:

- How am I dealing with the confusing issue?
- What other perspectives should I be listening to?
- What is happening around me right now?

By reflecting on the experience, you may generate insights that help you understand the ambiguous situation better or reframe the situation to give you a better perspective and allow you to connect to your past experiences and the environment you were in.

Participate in a 360° review. Executives are typically not very comfortable with being vulnerable at work or acknowledging blind spots, but they can gain insight from the organizational and environmental spheres. A 360° review can help you gain insight into the ambiguous situation.

Were you the subject or the object? Develop the basic process of developing a more complex mind and determining how you construct reality. The more realities you can see, the better able you are to respond and make decisions that make sense. By becoming more attuned to the subject-object concept, you will begin to surface your hidden assumptions about the world and others and achieve greater cognitive maturity in your personal and professional life.

Practice reflective journaling. You come to work with your own set of beliefs, principles, and values, and for the most part, you intend to go to work and do a good job. Unconsciously, when you are faced with dilemmas or stressful situations, you may project your own silo view onto others and narrow the solutions to your own insights. By finding negative thinking and behavior patterns through journaling, you may unblock a thinking or behavior barrier.

Ask your team for insights. Developing a structured and collective practice for uncertainty can be transformative. Involve your team in after-action reviews or lesson-learning exercises to find corporate value and opportunity. Each member of the team experienced the project differently, and by tapping into the meaning of each of their experiences, you will find ambiguity insights.

Engage in critical reflection. This is the process of reflecting on your experiences *and* learning from the experience *and* creating a behavior change.

. . . . .

CHAPTER 2

CULTIVATE ADAPTABLE MENTAL MODELS

A ll the interviewed executives expressed a need to have a fluid and dynamic thinking style that allowed them to question their own assumptions, and this learned skill is the second thinking and behavior strategy. Mental models are how you understand the world; they help you simplify complexity and build connections and frameworks in your head. There are many types of mental models that relate to guiding your perception and behavior when dealing in complexity and ambiguity. For example, there are the logical and causal mental models that help you understand the links between things by identifying the positive and negative correlations. There is also the model of inference, which uses your existing knowledge to develop a mental model of the most likely interpretation. Additional mental models include the following: model theory of deduction, and reasoning under uncertainty (Green, 1996).

It's important to note when your mental models are based on previous knowledge, and to understand how those perceptions can be expanded to cultivate adaptable mental models as part of an ambiguity mindset. Paying attention to your mental models can help you make wiser choices and take better actions.

A DEEP THINKING RUT

Despite the knowledge that mental models are not fixed and that you have the ability to expand your worldviews and obtain multiple perspectives, you still may get into thinking ruts. The thinking patterns that have served you well in normal and routine situations are familiar and comfortable, but they may not be the most effective approach in new or ambiguous situations. Moreover, even highly skilled and intellectual people who are in a role for a long time fall into something called a *competency trap*; they rely too heavily on their past experiences to solve future challenges.

The following is an exercise called "My Dinner Party" that pulls together the first two ambiguity thinking and behavior strategies—to create powerful critical reflection insights and to cultivate adaptable mental models.

Imagine that you're going to throw a dinner party and will invite eight of your closest family and friends. This dinner party is going to be a bit different, though. Instead of different food dishes, you are going to ask your family and friends to each bring a piece of personal or professional advice that they feel would benefit you. Your exercise is the following:

- List all the people you would invite to your dinner party.

- Write the advice you think each person would bring.

- Select the pieces of advice that resonate with you and seem beneficial to pursue.

- List the obvious barriers to achieving the newfound goals.

- List some ways to overcome the barriers to achieving the newfound goals.

- Write two positive phrases that create your new frame of reference.

- Now list your goals and the steps needed to achieve them.

You get advice from people, managers, and family all the time, but the advice is usually not presented in a way that allows you to give it serious consideration. You are focused on your own ways of completing tasks and objectives in your personal and professional life. The dinner party exercise can be completed by yourself or at an actual family or leadership workshop. I have completed this exercise at the beginning of the year when teams are completing their yearly objectives, because it helps shake loose old thinking habits about how to achieve goals and build a wider frame of opportunity for personal and professional growth. The most common phrase I hear from senior management when they complete this exercise is "Why is it so difficult to take on advice that you know is smart, helpful, and good for us?" A good question indeed.

Stubbornness is not necessarily a bad virtue, as Manfred Kets de Vries describes in "The Fine Line between Stubbornness and Stupidity" (Kets de Vries, 2018). However, a fixation on your own point of view—despite evidence that points to overwhelming contradictory information—is cause for a deliberate pause. Consider Isabella, who had been deemed stubborn by her peers. When the executive coach reviewed the psychometric assessment and the 360° review, the data showed that Isabella had strong opinions that rarely swayed. When asked about this observation, Isabella laughed and stated that she had always been called stubborn by her family, which indicated that this was not new or surprising information.

The paradox of being an executive is that you are privy to a large amount of high-level and confidential information that the team may not know about. Having a strong opinion is warranted and even expected. Only when the stubbornness may be part of confirmation bias, unconscious resistance to change, or deep-seated values of power and authority should a mindful conversation regarding leadership and, as Kets de Vries (2018) states, "the ugly side of stubbornness" take place.

Executives who learn to approach problems from different viewpoints leverage the context, paradoxes, tensions, and uniqueness of certain elements, which may also include their personal beliefs and assumptions and may allow new and creative ways to tackle messy or recurring issues. Reaffirming that an ambiguity mindset is largely a cognitive intellectual capability, it is important to cultivate the idea that you can expand your current perceptions—your wide-angle lens—to absorb the multitude of perspectives in your spheres of systems in order to make good decisions.

THINKING PRACTICES

Jean Piaget, a Swiss psychologist known for his work on the theory of cognitive development, described himself as a constructivist. A constructivist has the basic beliefs that not one explanation is ever possible, as windows of reality exist only in the context of a mental framework for thinking about it. Piaget recognized that learners construct new understandings and knowledge, integrating them with what they already know (Piaget, 1966). By including the other spheres of insight, your mental models are introduced to additional influencers. To build on that theory, Lev Vygotsky, a psychologist, stated that the nature of social constructivism emphasizes that all cognitive functions, including learning, are dependent on the interactions of others and are an active process (Vygotsky, 1978). Simply stated, you learn and continually enhance your mental models by paying attention to your interactions with your surroundings.

Social constructivists believe that knowledge is constructed when individuals engage on the social level with external learning factors that include cultural and social interactions. Carol Gilligan, professor of humanities and applied psychology at New York University, stated that relationships are like being on a trampoline; if one element changes, it resonates throughout. Gilligan viewed the world as a web of relationships and strongly advocated (from the women's viewpoint) for learning development within the interconnected relationships (Big Think, 2012). But when you are faced with unique situations, it is hard to make sense of all the interacting and paradox variables.

My executive interviews aligned with the premise that knowledge is created from understanding the networks, relationships, patterns, and mental models through a social constructivist approach. The executives displayed multiple viewpoints of the world, influenced by social, cultural, and language attributes. They explicitly mentioned an average of nine and a half times during the interview that they changed their viewpoints (or said something to that effect) on the basis of new information in order to think their way through ambiguous challenges. Adaptable mental models were part of their thinking DNA.

The executives tackled the uncertain and ambiguous issues that are prevalent within complex adaptive systems by assessing their own assumptions and beliefs. They questioned the structure of the issues to discover new or alternative ways of approaching the situation. This is called *double-loop* learning, coined by Argyris and Schön; it promotes the role of learning at the organizational level. In double-loop learning, long-held assumptions about systems and policies are challenged by questioning existing processes. The practice encourages system-wide thinking, continuous evaluation, and knowledge development (Argyris & Schön, 1974).

This concept has also been described in the workplace as doing a thing right versus doing the right thing. Double-loop learning involves collecting feedback from the experience that confronts your mental models and leads you to think in terms of different worldviews to seek opportunities for better processes, or to discover previously hidden information for continuous improvements (Argyris & Schön, 1974). Figure 5 shows how, for example, conflicting viewpoints in the workplace may arise. Some people may focus on the strategies and techniques of *what* needs to be completed. Other people may question deep assumptions of the process and ask *why* the process can't change to potentially get to a different but better result.

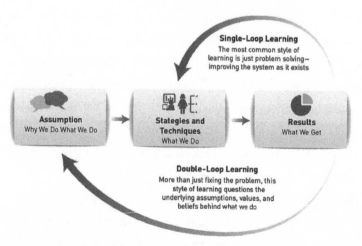

FIGURE 5. DOUBLE-LOOP LEARNING
(SOURCE: TROPICAL AGRICULTURE PLATFORM, 2016, p. 15)

Because of constant shifts within complex adaptive systems, it is essential to have insights that essentially allow you to see around corners to understand the interactions within the individual, organizational, and environmental spheres. Simple solutions rarely work in the face of significant complexity. Taking a deliberate pause to implement double-loop learning when faced with recurring issues can take you toward a more sustainable and better solution.

Flexible mental models may enable you to see all parts of the organization and environment rather than focus on the issues as they arise. Our health care executive, Amy, stated, "I think a lot. I've always been open to challenges and to learning and changing my viewpoint. If presented with new information, I would change my mind."

All the executives expressed a need to have a fluid and dynamic thinking style that allowed them to question their own assumptions. Karim, who is always conducting both formal and informal learning situations, stated, "When meeting the new chairman for our client for the first time, I realized that the relationship wasn't going to work as expected because we had two different thinking styles. But I noticed in the first meeting that my junior partner was able to resonate better with the chairman, who was clearly relating to him. I concluded that my junior partner was going to be more of an efficient counterpart to frame and channel our exchanges with the chairman. I simply wasn't the right person to drive this agenda."

Rachid, the oil and gas executive, described an experience in which a complex government issue caused him a huge temporary setback. Feeling a lack of control, Rachid reflected on the situation and eventually presented a unique solution to the government, which it approved. During and after the experience, he felt the need to make a personal shift in thinking to make meaning of the experience. "I was forced to become humble. Definitely, a mindset shift was required."

When nudged into a different mindset, you may feel as if your identity has been unpleasantly attacked. This is due to your perceived need to hang on to your preexisting beliefs. The key is to recognize when your viewpoint may be based on emotion, affiliation, assumption, bias, or simply a hard-nosed belief in a fact that may not be compatible with the context or situation.

During my research, I noted that many of the executives identified moments of learning within a certain context, such as their upbringing, and reflected on that context to create meaning. They pointed to key experiences that may have helped them develop a dynamic mental model. This included the information and technology executive, Karim, who started the interview by stating, "I was born, schooled, and did my undergraduate and graduate studies in Lebanon during the time of the civil war [1975–1990]. Growing up in this environment teaches you early on how to make critical decisions with limited information. While I do not wish for anyone to go through such a learning process, it taught me early how to make decisions with limited data, such as, 'Is it safe to go to school today? How will I access the university campus if the checkpoint is closed? How will I access the computer lab if the power is down?' The constantly changing situation on the ground teaches you the value of dynamic thinking."

Throughout your life, you are continually picking up thinking and behavior patterns from your environment to expand your mental models, and in this case, Karim was adjusting to continually changing and risky situations while still a young adult.

Organizational psychologists use the concept of *the self as an instrument* to be the thermometer to assess conditions, dive into their own and other people's perceptions, understand bias, postpone judgment, and attempt to capture the experience. These attributes allow you to assess the initial hypothesis and to continually review and reflect on the discussions, conflicts, disinterest, and other typical organizational behaviors that accompany any change project. The benefits of using yourself as an instrument are to increase your awareness of situations and to attempt to improve any miscalculations.

BEHAVIOR PRACTICES

The executives' narratives all pointed to the same three key aspects of their cognitive learning architecture in their adaptive mental models. These included seeking meaning and adopting sensemaking attributes, promoting critical dialogue, and fostering crucial connections.

SEEKS MEANING AND SENSEMAKING ATTRIBUTES

In *Sensemaking in Organizations*, Karl Weick stated that employees build a sensemaking capacity with new or unique information when there are no past experiences to build frames of reference (Weick, 1995). Meryl Reis Louis, a professor at UCLA whose research concerned socialization of new members into unfamiliar organizational settings, described sense making as the "thinking process that uses retrospective accounts to explain surprises" and further explained that "sense making can be viewed as a recurring cycle of a sequence of events" (Louis, 1980, p. 241).

Weick stated that sensemaking attributes involve coming up with a plausible understanding and then testing this understanding with others by collecting data, action, and conversation and then refining it—or abandoning it, depending on how credible it is (Weick, 1995). The cycle begins as the individuals form an unconscious or conscious assumption, which serves as a prediction about future events. Sensemaking properties may help augment your mental models and serve as key components to help you understand more about ambiguity thinking and behavior strategies.

One of the key elements of an ambiguity mindset identified from our interview narratives was the premise of turning thinking strategies into thinking actions. Being able and willing to understand or at least to be curious about the premise of learning from your experiences, learning from your own and others' behaviors, and embracing the importance of context to turn information into knowledge—these are all important behavioral attributes.

William Starbuck and Frances Milliken describe the ability to make sense as to "structure the unknown, to comprehend, understand, explain, attribute, extrapolate, and predict" (Starbuck & Milliken, 1988). It's also critical to be able to understand cause-effect relationships in projects that involve large time delays. This is difficult in complex adaptive systems because of the changing people and behaviors involved. The real estate executive—Adam—described a situation in which he conducted sense making: "I was in a difficult situation, as we were asked to do a very big problematic project, and since direct communication was also problematic, I needed to feel around the edges, read between the lines, and see the wider context. There was no pathway, and it was one of those things where you need to read the signals and symptoms to figure out what is happening."

All the executives I interviewed mentioned trying to make meaning of events so they could identify plausible explanations when an event surprised them. This was evident with the entrepreneurial executive—Hazel—who stated, "You know, I suppose my opening point is just being really curious and asking a whole load of questions. I am typically less curious about what happened or how it happened but more about why it happened."

By being curious, the executives promoted a continuous learning journey that allowed them to understand the changing landscape, connections, and relationships, creating an opportunity for various positive feedback loops. The renewable energy executive—Charlie—seeks meaning from patterns of information. He stated, "I am an information addict. I always collect all kinds of information, and I have, like, these different piles on my desk and different folders and am always learning all kinds of stuff. It's just natural curiosity, but I never know exactly why I need it."

Similarly, Karim, the information and technology executive, was also trying to construct meaning. "The right model for me is to learn about and develop a certain model, adopt, and continuously evolve it. You have to be obsessed with the idea of constant evolution in order to achieve continuous progress." Adam had a similar take, based on his background in real estate. He said, "You have to accept that there's always a better solution, and maybe this includes being open or having a mindset that there's always something to learn. You can be stubborn about something and insist that it is the only way, but I don't think that gets you very far."

Complex adaptive systems contain paradoxes, rapid changes, and dynamic forces that cause knowledge to become quickly obsolete. Through the concept of sense making, Rachid, the oil and gas executive, stated that by being resilient and linking threads of information, your thinking patterns can become clearer: "I solved the ambiguous situation myself with a little bit of chance and a little bit of pointing in the right direction and insisting on it. Sometimes when you feel grumpy and upset, maybe that is the fuel that is required to point you in a specific direction to keep you resilient."

A bit of sense making and planned happenstance may help uncover hidden thinking and behavior pathways to deal with ambiguity. Consider the Stanford professors John Krumboltz and Al Levin, who developed the planned happenstance learning theory to help students make connections and plan for change. Essentially, they found that five traits best helped students: curiosity, persistence, flexibility, optimism, and risk taking (Krumboltz & Levin, 2004). The goal was to encourage students to examine new events as opportunities and to discover what's possible when they're in the right place at the right time with the right tools.

Adam, our real estate executive, explained that to detect nuances, he learned to look for more information from all organizational levels. He said, "You eventually may need to develop your own interpretation on the situation, and there's something about being in the right place at the right time." When faced with unique learning situations, by applying sensemaking attributes and making meaning from experiences that occur in the individual, organizational, and environmental spheres—as well as some happenstance—you can prepare yourself mentally for unpredictable events. This helps you begin to discover a framework to tackle the uncertain pathway.

PROMOTES CRITICAL DIALOGUE

Complex adaptive systems involve a holistic view of a system that contains fluid and dynamic feedback loops that connect to the changing environment. No single person can understand the entire system, and embracing diversity of thought, perspectives, and viewpoints is critical for developing an ambiguity mindset. Leveraging information through critical dialogue helps you uncover heuristics to create a broader platform of ideas.

Amy, the health care executive, explained how meeting with different people to view a problem from multiple viewpoints provided her with a better understanding of the root cause issue. She stated, "They have different skill sets, and they complement each other. To have one person calling all the shots would not give a holistic picture." Charlie, the renewable energy executive, added, "You can actually discover new territory and create something new. It's usually not driven by numbers; it's determined by a group of people trying to aspire [to] something and willing to go on a path of discovery rather than 'What do I know.'" Promoting critical dialogue encourages systems-wide thinking. Your attention is placed on information from multiple sources, essentially revealing the relationships and networks between the parts—the departments—rather than solely domain-specific information.

According to Argyris and Schön, being able to detect and correct errors in organizations is more than following norms or rules; it requires critically questioning the operating norms (Argyris & Schön, 1974). Henry Mintzberg, a professor of management at McGill University, wrote many articles on business strategy and claimed that the key flexibility of executives' mental models is their ability to question their deeply held perspectives of the world. "Every manager has a mental model of the world in which he or she acts based on experience and knowledge. However, it is difficult to question one's own assumptions in isolation" (Mintzberg, 1994, p. 368).

The executives all provided evidence of critical dialogue as an important factor while describing a significant learning moment. This is more than just placing effort on good communications; it's about placing more emphasis on creating situations that blend interactions for the purpose of sharing information about the issues at hand. Charlie, the renewable energy executive, was emphatic that innovation does not work without critical discussion exploring different viewpoints. He explained that building a corporate culture that integrates this discussion practice, such as brainstorming sessions, is part of the important learning journey: "You've got to rely on people, and by doing that, you create a culture of solution-based thinking. You create a learning environment that allows those learning moments to occur."

As a real estate executive, Adam uses dialogue to avoid short-term thinking. He said, "When the team is facing a big, uncertain project, sometimes you have to explain it to them in a long story to avoid them having a knee-jerk reaction to the uncertainty. I try to pull back the immediate reaction, go for a walk with them, and drink a cup of coffee to discuss the situation. You need to invest time in them."

John Dewey claimed that critical inquiry was one of the main elements of being able to learn from experience, and the concept of team inquiry–based dialogue is widely used and referenced within organizational learning theory (Dewey, 1938). More information can be gleaned through direct interactions, which are a form of extracting tacit knowledge from individuals and converting it to explicit knowledge. Through dialogue and interactions, the executives were challenging routine ways of communicating and increasing their potential of uncovering unknown knowledge through interactions.

Karim, our information and technology executive, supported this theory, saying, "I try to reach out to the guys who probably are the most insightful. They are probably not the highest in the hierarchy, but generally, they are the people who would be excited about telling you how things work. Then you start listening and learning about the alternative models."

Extraneous factors force the executives into seeking information; their narratives indicate that critical dialogue is essential. For example, Michael, a hospitality investment executive, put it this way: "If we were able to do x, y, z, then perhaps we could achieve this outcome. When you're searching for a solution to a different answer, then you need to involve a whole range of different people." Additionally, Charlie stated that learning about knowledge sharing early in his career helped him learn to navigate through uncertain situations: "You have the social intelligences. You have the people like me, who could recognize patterns and somehow translate and communicate that. You had people who were just brains; they could mathematically do anything. You certainly gain an appreciation for it. Hey, if you put this all together, you could do anything in the world—literally—because you covered all the bases. That gave me real insight."

In addition, Hazel, our entrepreneurial interviewee, embraced group questioning to uncover information, perspectives, and understanding: "You know, I have spent entire meetings asking questions. I try to ask more questions to get perspectives."

FOSTERS CRUCIAL CONNECTIONS

The third relevant action-oriented behavior description elicited from the executive narratives was fostering crucial connections. As they described it, the executives placed emphasis on the people within the environment to create crucial connections to enhance the inquiry process. The information and technology executive, Karim, explained the ideal plan for any complex or uncertain situation that needed to be addressed: "The objective is to recruit the best minds in the industry. Each of these individuals comes with essential knowledge. When they join communities of interest, they start shaping the capabilities systems that markedly impact the way we deliver solutions in the market. This system also starts exploring new ways of doing things, triggering constant evolution."

Other executives explored their perspectives and their environment through the crucial connections that are required for any situation. Charlie, the renewable energy executive, continued to explain how understanding the team, in all its diversity, is strongly recommended before a solution can be reached. "I'm obviously just trying to get another person's perspective," he said. "I'm trying to find the empathy, the anchor points which can help me to create a language with that particular person, or group of people. I want to determine what the cultural inheritance is and where the mandate is, where you are crossing the lines. You have to map out the person before you go into how you are going to translate it to complexity. I'm very much into this self-reflective loop: finding the right work, then doing the work right. The crux of this is really based on connecting with people."

Although cognitive reasoning supports changes to flexible thinking, enhancing processes involves other people, elements, and influencers to correct an error or organizational issue.

A wide-angle lens includes building a network of learning relationships that emphasizes an ambiguity mindset. Jean Lave and Etienne Wenger, adult learning and development theorists, described this type of learning as part of the community of practice model for situated learning (Lave & Wenger, 1991). Learning arises from participation in the wider social network. For example, Amy, our health care executive, stated, "I like the excitement, the unpredictability, the comradery, the collaboration. This is always about a team."

The hospitality executive in the group, Michael, described a large-scale complex issue that required collaboration from a diverse group to think through a new way of doing things: "So, you always get the enthusiasm of youth and the experience of someone who's been around a while. And they are considered sort of equal, so everyone's opinion had to be listened to. It encouraged discussion."

The executives placed considerable value on nurturing the relationships within the network to uncover disconnects and to understand, which is difficult in complex global entities but considered integral to developing an ambiguity mindset. Shipping executive Marcus stated, "We all have a sort of common language we do in business, regardless of whether your friends are Canadian or Dutch or Emirati. There are always forces at play, I guess—politics and other elements of socioeconomics that are not immediately visible." The executives exhibited the ability to be more aware of how, through their experiential learning lens, to step outside of their potentially dominant ideology or culturally determined perspective to craft new ideas or alternative perspectives.

The executives also indicated that connections within the organization or their network were crucial for a diversity of thought and aided in problem solving. Connections have a positive impact on creative thinking, especially within complex adaptive systems. Ambiguous situations have self-organizing agents within subsystems, and problems are fluid. A necessary condition for overcoming or recovering from disturbances is to develop deep connections throughout the organization to determine the next decision. The renewable energy executive, Charlie, explained how understanding people is more important than understanding the process. "Once you realize the work package is a really pathetic way to help people get things done, you can hop into a different paradigm and say, 'Well, let's aspire to do something. What do we have? What do we need?' If you maintain mutual benefit constantly, then things tend to self-organize. If you are conscious that we are in this together, you get something and create that value."

Information and technology executive Karim was equally supportive of fostering connections to progress a project. "Complex situations are often unlocked through conversations. Through these fluid exchanges, you get a sense of what is important and build on the different viewpoints. Solving problems by trading documented briefings is too static as a process."

Rachid, the oil and gas executive, agreed: "I think, with buy-in and winning people over, working on your partner's journey, that part of your journey is critical." To ease the journey toward learning how to develop an ambiguity mindset, seek to ensure you embrace sensemaking attributes, promote critical dialogue, and foster crucial connections.

LEADERSHIP GAPS

Consider Robert, who has worked for three years at an innovative technology company located in the Middle East. He is a seasoned and successful expert in his field, having worked in the military on information technology and security for over two decades. Robert fills a room with his presence; he is over six feet tall and has a dynamic personality, a big laugh, and a loud, booming voice.

In the three years that Robert ran the IT department that was undergoing dynamic changes, he felt that he had assimilated well into the private sector and added value through his experiences and success at hitting annual targets. Imagine his surprise when he got a call from HR for a meeting. It seems there had been numerous complaints from his direct reports and peers concerning his strategic execution, communication, and team management skills. Robert thought that he had already addressed his mannerisms and made adjustments when he transitioned from his military job, so he was completely shocked and confused by the complaints. He was sure it was because the team members were worried about their upcoming performance meetings and were seeking HR's assistance before they received their performance feedback. However, Robert felt obligated to meet with the executive coach as HR requested.

When Robert met the executive coach, the coach mentioned the following issues about Robert that had been raised in the HR meeting. Although Robert did not believe these were actual issues, he wanted to follow protocol. HR had listed these as his areas of opportunity to improve:

- Weak engagement skills and effectiveness
- Ineffective communication patterns
- Limitations on strategic execution

During the discussion, Robert was asked to describe his identity and how he thought others perceived him. He described himself as a mentally strong person who is fair, a hard worker, and generous with his time to help others learn from his vast experiences. When the coach asked him to further describe how he thought and behaved during times of stress, Robert admitted that he might default to being very rational and logical, with a laser focus on the outcomes, and might have, on occasion, given direct orders to his team that may have sounded harsh. When he was asked to describe how he thought others perceived him as a person and a leader, Robert needed to ponder this question for a moment, but he was sure that people described him as he saw himself: fair, knowledgeable, and proficient in his job.

During the coaching session, Robert explored what is meaningful and important in his role and how he can create a behavioral solution that is significant for himself, his peers, and his direct reports. Robert was able to reflect on his behaviors and how he interpreted his interactions during ambiguous workplace situations. He became aware that he'd been focused only on his own work path rather than on bringing other people along on the learning journey. He then embraced the *adaptable mental models* behavior strategy to become better able to understand what is happening in his environment and his team dynamics to become a better leader.

What Robert learned about himself and his team during the course of the sessions was that he really didn't know his team at all during constant workplace change, despite working together for over three years. He was unaware of their motivations, their hidden behaviors, and their insecurities.

Although feedback can be difficult to hear, after speaking with the coach, Robert conducted one-on-one meetings with his team. He listened quietly as each of his team members asked (in a variety of different ways) for a different kind of support and guidance. He became aware of how his emotions, behaviors, and actions were actually scaring his team into silence and obedience rather than helping them develop into a dynamic team with new insights, autonomy, and accountability. It is no wonder his communication skills (in his individual sphere) were affecting his team's engagement levels (in the organizational sphere) and his ability to execute the strategic plan (in the environmental sphere). Robert was overconfident in his leadership skills when facing new situations and realized that his past militaristic, entrenched behaviors were incongruent with the fluid work environment.

Through further discussion with the executive coach, Robert began learning about the ambiguity decoding principles: perspective taking, learning more about your own and other people's thinking and behavior patterns, and seeking meaning from your situational experiences. By expanding his perspective into the outer spheres—the organizational and environmental space—Robert began to understand why context matters and how his own mental models may not have been an accurate depiction of the situation. He needed to develop an ambiguity mindset to address his not-so-new context and to dissolve his blind spots.

Biases are easier to spot in others than they are in yourself. Through your lack of awareness, you may be unintentionally judging people and situations, and you are making assumptions that may affect your response to events around you. The good news is that in most situations, how you think and make assumptions in your life may be accurate as you see and learn in your environment, infer the problem, and then draw a conclusion. But as you probably know, your assumptions can sometimes lead you to incorrect conclusions, and this can cause issues, especially when your assumptions are wrong about interpersonal relationships and other people's intentions.

Remember Carter, who yelled at his team and called them lazy? A fundamental attribution error is when you tend to assume that an observed behavior of another person is simply a trait and underestimate the power of the situation on their behavior. Carter assumed that missed deadlines, fatigue, and a lack of enthusiasm meant that his team was lazy, but all these issues stemmed from his abrasive leadership style. Was Carter a mean, angry, or rude man? More than likely, Carter's behavior could be explained by an external factor or situation—the context.

LADDER OF INFERENCE

Chris Argyris (1982) developed a model called the ladder of inference as a double-loop learning tool to help people reflect on their behavior and to process the reasoning behind it, especially when you make assumptions about the intentions or beliefs of others (see Figure 6).

FIGURE 6. LADDER OF INFERENCE
(SOURCE: SYSTEMS THINKER, 2009)

Consider Kim, a midlevel manager who is worried about her upcoming yearly performance review, and since she has been with the company for over three years, she is expecting her big promotion this year. But Kim is a bit worried that the promotion might not happen, as only a few people can get promoted each year.

RUNG 1: OBSERVE DATA

The first rung on the ladder is selecting *observable data*: This is the information that you see, hear, or notice about your surroundings. In Kim's case, it's promotion time, and her manager has not discussed a performance review with her yet. The observable data is the time frame (yearly reviews), her desire for a promotion, and the fact that her manager has not yet discussed a meeting. Kim might say, "It's promotion time, and my manager has not discussed any performance review with me yet."

RUNG 2: MAKE ASSUMPTIONS

Rung 2 is paraphrasing the data, or making *assumptions*. Once Kim has the data (performance review time and no meeting scheduled), Kim naturally starts to filter the information through her thinking patterns and what she understands from her previous experiences. Kim might conclude she is not on the promotion list because she thinks (assumption) that her manager also wants a promotion. "I don't think I am on the promotion list, as my manager also wants a promotion. She will not promote me."

RUNG 3: DRAW CONCLUSIONS

Next, Kim names what's happening, or draws *conclusions*. Kim assigns meaning or interprets the information from all the assumptions that she formed about the situation. "I have spent three years with this company, and they don't care about their employees. I bet my manager will get a promotion and not me, as promotions are given to 'who you are,' rather than 'what you do.'"

RUNG 4: ADOPT BELIEFS

Rung 4 is evaluating what's happening, to *adopt beliefs*. This is where Kim turns her conclusion into beliefs. When Kim forms her beliefs, she may go back to the data and selectively reassess the information to coincide with her assumptions and conclusions. Or she might disregard crucial observable data and reach incorrect assumptions. "My manager is jealous of me, and that's why she won't promote me."

RUNG 5: TAKE ACTION

On rung 5, Kim decides to *take action*. She might act on her created beliefs and assumptions by making rash decisions. "I will go to HR myself and request my promotion, as my manager is incompetent."

You have all been there. You have made assumption after assumption without any evidence when rushed to make a decision with either limited information or multiple options. When you are at the top of the ladder taking action, it is hard to see how you got there. You may not be able to see past your beliefs, assumptions, and conclusions to the primary data on the bottom rung. It's promotion time, and you haven't had a meeting yet, which is far from warranting a meeting with HR. The goal is to get off the ladder and focus on good communication. Test out your assumptions by discussing the data with other people. The easiest first step here would be for Kim to ask her manager about the performance meeting.

To avoid running up the ladder of inference, reflect on your own thinking process (your understanding and reasoning). You can make your thinking and reasoning more visible to others by speaking up and labeling the situation as you see it. Then, you inquire into the other party's thinking process by asking and being curious. Otherwise, you may get tripped up on your incorrect assumptions and can easily hurt yourself (or your career) by falling off the top of the ladder.

This model can be used for advocacy and inquiry and to check the steps used in your own reasoning. Look for information that challenges your own and others' assumptions, and be aware of how your actions become information for others. Argyris's work was instrumental on how to make decisions; it can be helpful when one is immersed in ambiguity. Your assumptions, values, and beliefs contribute to the ambiguity within the system.

Here are some good questions to ask yourself to ensure you are not racing to the top of the ladder based only on assumptions:

- What is going on? (Seek the real data.)

- How do I understand the situation? What assumptions have I made?

- What was my reasoning that led from the original data to my assumptions

Then, ask questions of the other people involved:

- How do you see the situation? (That is, how does their observed data differ from yours?)

- When you said this, did you mean that? (Check your interpretation of the data.)

This will start you on the path to a clearer conversation. You'll be up front with your interpretation of the data and can replace your assumptions with new, more informed data before taking any action.

Key Takeaways

Be curious. You must make the effort and take the time to be curious, ask questions, test your assumptions, and seek alternative viewpoints. Employees tend not to ask many questions and, instead, move forward with potentially misguided action. Taking the time to gain a holistic view of the situation slows down the rapid short-term decision-making process just enough to seek other points of view to reach a more sustainable decision. It is humbling but essential to develop the ability to ask questions and to know that you don't need to be the expert in the room.

Seek information outside of your immediate sphere. Develop ways to communicate with people. Seek information from a diverse group of people to gain other perspectives. This does not just mean from different departments; it includes people of different nationalities, upbringings, and age groups.

Move toward double-loop learning. If you have solved problems the way you've always solved them, you may find that a routine solution—a single-loop solution—is somewhat ineffective for an ambiguous situation. You often cannot solve a complex issue with a simple solution. Single-loop learning is accepting the set structure, policies, and practices to address problems, whereas to move toward the double-loop learning method, you must challenge the underlying assumptions of the problem to find the root cause, reflect on the previous experiences, and question the process. Double-loop learning is thinking more deeply about your own and others' assumptions of how things should be done. It requires you to transform your thinking about the way you seek solutions.

Use adaptive mental models. Feedback is one of the most crucial tools in being able to assess your own mental models and to see how others' mental models interact with your own worldview. If you have ever been given performance feedback that you need to collaborate more, the intent may be that you need greater insights for the team to hone your own insights into better decisions. You must be able to view your world through multiple lenses in order to make sound decisions. When you make unilateral decisions, you may create more issues or waste time by not taking into account the entire system of events, perspectives, and outcomes. Seeking an executive coach can be helpful in understanding your mental models.

Avoid racing up the ladder of inference. If you have ever found yourself surprised by someone's actions or offended by their comments, you have probably just climbed the ladder of inference. To avoid this and to help others avoid it as well, you can continue to draw on your experiences but in a way that does not include assumptions about other people's behaviors. You must check in with the data—ask them about it. Be curious, ask questions, and try to understand how the other person perceives the experience.

Three ways to cultivate adaptable mental models are to seek meaning and adopt sensemaking attributes, foster crucial connections, and promote critical dialogue.

· · · · · ·

CHAPTER 3

DEVELOP COMFORT IN THE UNKNOWN

The foundation of cognitive complexities is based on the mental structures you can develop to analyze a situation, perceive nuances, and explore the connections to make decisions. People with high cognitive complexity are able to detect clues where none are obvious, think through complex layers of information, understand behaviors with more acuity than others, and better perceive and respond to variables based on their prior experiences. However, this foundation requires specific behaviors to create the experiences that build expertise. An overwhelming amount of interview coded research pointed to the fact that the executives seek out challenging environments, placing themselves in situations to learn alternative ways of thinking and to challenge their assumptions, to ultimately learn to develop a comfort in the unknown, the third thinking and behavior strategy.

In early studies on tolerating ambiguity, Else Frenkel-Brunswik made multiple attempts to measure ambiguity behaviors on a scale. For example, in one study, she learned that those who were intolerant of ambiguity were usually described as people who made fast-paced black-and-white decisions and were characterized as overconfident, whereas at the other end of the scale were those who perceived ambiguous situations as interesting and challenging and were characterized as risk takers (Frenkel-Brunswik, 1949).

Today, there are many psychometric tools to assess a person's comfort level in making difficult decisions along a spectrum. If you have ever completed this type of assessment, you will know that no matter which end of the comfort scale your behavior preferences fall on, there are still a variety of coping mechanisms you need to be cognizant of. For example, you might be a quick decision maker in the absence of all the information. Although this type of behavior may be a valuable trait in certain circumstances, it might also cause issues if the decisions are not the right ones to make. Similarly, if you are cautious and like to have as much information as possible before making a decision, you may be viewed as practical, but it may also stall corporate projects.

THE KNOWING GAP

Being able to recognize a knowing gap and continually seeking information from the spheres of insight is part of the process of developing an ambiguity mindset. It would be reasonable to assume you know at least one person—a smart person—who may be an expert in their field but who seems to bumble through other aspects of their life. They don't seem to pick up on certain subtle clues regarding situations, behaviors, or relationships. The common joke may be something like "Omar is the dumbest smart person I know." This deep domain knowledge is an important indication of that person's expertise. If you remember, this is the third decoding principle: Develop the ability to learn from your experiences, seek clues from your surroundings, and absorb the world's fluid elements to make effective decisions to become more comfortable with ambiguity.

A common example of the knowing gap is an employee in isolation. Let's say Reema from HR sits fewer than fifty steps from Naya in finance. Neither person knows their colleague's full name or the details of the job they're doing. Furthermore, their department teams don't mingle in the hallways or eat lunch together. It is difficult for a business to force you to share information; you need to learn how to discover knowledge for yourself. Consider a company that started to conduct "lunch and learn" sessions with managers from different departments after noticing ineffective transfer of information between departments. At first it surprised the facilitator that managers walked into the session and introduced themselves to other participants, meeting for the first time—after working in the same midsize company for years. Yet they were complete strangers.

They were strangers because each person was focused on their own job from their own space and made little to no effort to know the other aspects of the business, much less its people. If this is happening in your company, you should be worried about misalignment of goals and activities. Narrow thinking leads to errors and costly missed opportunities. Companies perpetuate this situation by reinforcing department silos, which can dissolve strategic alignment as the connective links and corporate learning opportunities become weak.

Unfortunately, you may also have observed multiple examples of both major and minor issues in which an executive fell into the knowing gap by failing to recognize nuances or social cues or to understand the complexity of a problem. The reason this happens is simple: It takes effort and time to be the corporate connector—the person who seeks information, asks questions, and learns the nuances of the system and people's behavior patterns.

Sharing knowledge in a business is a critical tool and is more difficult than most leaders believe. Consider two executives with different knowledge-sharing behaviors. One would spend the first hour of each morning walking around the office and having conversations with different managers. The other executive would go straight to their desk and speak to people only when they needed to, essentially avoiding small talk and office conversations. Over time, you could see that the first executive was far more successful at understanding the company, innovating, and executing on collaborative projects, while the other executive was destined to be an information taker, exhibiting only linear tactical skills.

While not ideal, there are executives who can't find time to conduct team meetings. Executives are extremely busy with urgent requirements; however, the knowing gap only grows wider when there are no direct or frequent communication mechanisms in place. As Leonardo, one of the interview executives who works in private equity, put it, "There's always pros and cons for everything. If your team leaves you alone, you can focus. So, there is an advantage. But one has to be careful, because isolation is very dangerous."

Compounding the issue, less emphasis is placed on informal learning—harvesting knowledge from small daily interactions—and on verifying whether those small moments are valuable. Informal learning is difficult to measure, and you don't always know when learning is taking place. Sometimes you can't even determine which experiences are meaningful. Many people still believe that you can learn new principles, concepts, and theories only within a classroom.

The ambiguity mindset does not have a predefined learning path. That's the point. By learning how to shift the way you think, you can be prepared for any situation, no matter how ambiguous. Understanding more about the types of experiences you might face will also help.

THINKING PRACTICES

According to Eric Vogt (1995), how individuals learn (the process) and why they learn (the context) may be more important than what they learn (the content). Leveraging this concept, you can create a mindset blueprint based on how you draw on your own past experiences, make inferences, and understand different perceptions to make informed decisions.

Professor Lyle Yorks, from Columbia University, and Professor Aliki Nicolaides, from the University of Georgia, wrote about the implications of the intensifying complexity confronting adults in their personal and professional lives. Their article includes some narratives from two adult students on how they became more aware of their own learning strategies during times of ambiguity. One of the students was confounded by the need to learn on his own. For example, he thought he was being duped and expressed his concern as, "Are you saying that it is my role to learn how to learn from you by learning how I learn from myself? You mean to say that your role [as a teacher] is not to teach me what to learn?" (Yorks & Nicolaides, 2013).

However, throughout the program, the students began to realize that they were in charge of their own experiences, and they learned how to create meaning from them. Another student was part of the senior management team of her company and prided herself on her pointed, linear, self-directed, and motivated way of tackling her learning. She discovered that, in her push to know, she was missing potential opportunities. She said, "Innately, I am a linear thinker, but through this class, I had to learn how to engage in a more spiral, paradoxical thinking. I had to learn how to be in a relationship with the unpredictable and uncertain realities of strategy, how to feel empowered by ambiguity. It was only after much struggle that I experienced a shift in my mindset" (Yorks & Nicolaides, 2013).

Passive learning—moving from experience to experience without paying attention or outright disregarding cues that enable better decision-making—is not conducive to becoming more comfortable with the unknown. Yorks and Nicolaides support that transformative learning and adaptive leadership connection. They reiterate, "Learning experiences that develop an awareness of one's mindset and its impact on one's thinking and acting under conditions of ambiguity and uncertainty is critical" (Yorks & Nicolaides, 2013, p. 4).

DEMYSTIFYING THE UNKNOWN

The other interviewed health care executive, Lynn, worked in the emergency room for a time, which certainly offers conditions of ambiguity. She stated, "Ambiguity is actually something in nursing and in medicine that we talk about quite frequently. It's just one of those things that nobody particularly likes, because it's uncomfortable. Medicine and nursing are a science that likes certainty, and it's built on knowing or trying to know the exact answer to things—how cancer affects the body and how diseases progress. So with ambiguity, it sucks, and it makes us uncomfortable, because we don't know what's going to happen, and we don't know how to deal with something. But once you allow yourself into the uncertainty feeling, you become okay with it, and then you have the ability to say, 'I don't really know what's going to happen, but let's talk about it.' I think I built this learning capacity by being in an environment that is very collaborative, learning from others, and seeing how others react in those situations."

Our interviewed executives made only a few references to their feelings or emotional state when they were faced with ambiguity. A few mentioned having feelings of frustration with certain troublesome issues or felt humbled when they experienced painful mind shifts and thinking errors. However, the absence of explicit narratives on the executives' feelings should not be overlooked; I suspect there were stressful times in which the fight-or-flight mechanism was in play.

When you are immersed in a very stressful situation where you might not know the next step, what are you feeling? Is your heart racing? Are you full of fear and anxiety? Developing an emotional comfort in the unknown is no easy task. Think back to Carter, who shouted at his team when confronted by an unusual situation. By learning more about your emotional triggers, you can help control your anxiety, fear, and stress.

As a quick exercise, go back to your reflective journaling. I hope that you have been monitoring your emotional state when describing potentially difficult moments. If you have not started journaling yet, think back to the last uncertain situation you experienced. What was your emotional state during the confusion? Now, how did you calm yourself down? What elements helped you tackle the situation? List all the coping mechanisms you used to think your way out of the messy situation.

If your last reaction was less than ideal, you will need to understand more about emotional intelligence during times of uncertainty. Emotional intelligence is a set of emotional and social skills that influence the way we perceive and express ourselves, develop and maintain social relationships, cope with challenges, and use emotional information in an effective and meaningful way.

Emotional intelligence is widely referenced when talking about systems thinking, mental models, and learning from experience. It involves the ability to recognize your own emotions, as well as the emotions of other people. Those emotions change through dynamic situations and influence your thinking and behavior. If you have ever reflected on your wild emotions during a relationship breakup or at being passed over for a promotion, you will remember how your emotions may have superseded rational thought. Being able to recognize, understand, and learn how to manage your emotions is a giant piece of the dynamic puzzle of learning through the three spheres of insight.

The International Coaching Federation is the regulatory body for certifying professional executive coaches. It provides a variety of tools and resources that coaches use as part of their practice. One of those practices is to let the client be in a learning and reflective space. Coaches create a space without conversation, without questions, and let the clients reflect on a discussion point. Lynn, the health care executive, called it *being present*. She said, "Being present doesn't mean that you have to keep talking and make the patient feel better. Being present is just being in the moment with the patient, helping them feel safe, letting them know that they can cry, that they can talk, and that they can express whatever is going on with them at the moment." When you are faced with emotional information, let yourself be present and reflect on the emotions and the coping mechanisms that have previously enabled you to remain calm when faced with ambiguity.

Neuroscience also plays a part in demystifying ambiguity. David Rock, cofounder and chief executive officer of the NeuroLeadership Institute, says that "neural connections can be re-formed, new behaviors can be learned, and even the most entrenched behaviors can be modified at any age" (Rock, 2009, p. 7).

Understanding the basic neuroscience of learning and of dealing with complex challenges can help you integrate the principles of mindful attention. You can create a wide learning path for your organization and develop initiatives that enable your executives to be mindful of the patterns of their thoughts and feelings. As they work toward developing greater self-awareness and reflective practices, they will develop the cognitive skills for confronting ambiguity.

The executives' abilities to manage their emotions and change their behaviors are important factors when dealing with ambiguity. Kathleen

Taylor and Catherine Marienau, authors of *Facilitating Learning with the Adult Brain in Mind*, state, "The human brain is a social organ and organizes prior experiences in ways that enables an individual to revisit and reconsider them, thus gaining the benefits of hindsight, specifically reflection for learning. The brain is also hardwired to understand feedback in unique ways, and positive and negative feedback and our response to it can create stress, anxiety, fear, or happiness" (Taylor & Marienau, 2016, p. 215).

The use of analogies has been supported as a strategy when working within complex problems and conditions of uncertainty. Making an analogy is a cognitive process in which a piece of known information is linked to the dilemma, which helps conjure up a mental picture of something that is not easily visualized. Such comparisons are usually two unrelated objects compared for their shared qualities and are helpful to bridge the knowledge or understanding gap. The executives used analogies frequently when describing their ambiguous experiences.

Adam, our real estate executive, described chaos through an analogy. "I think a lot of times, you get all worked up about what is going on around you and get too immersed in the craziness of the situation. I just try to find my perspective again and zoom in on what you can control. It's like going through a butterfly garden, and once you go inside, you see all the butterflies going in every direction. Everywhere you look, it looks random and chaotic. But if you take a moment and sit on the bench and take in what is happening, you will end up with the butterflies perched on and around you. So, you don't need to look at the ten thousand different butterflies at the same time. You can just calm down and learn through the craziness." Leaning into ambiguous situations is how you shift to an ambiguity mindset.

I assume you've had moments where you were in a meeting and something unexpected happened that caught you off guard. Although you prepared for the ideal scenario, you may not have prepared your mind for when things go wrong. How would you feel in this situation? Are you in a state of paralysis, fear, or confidence? Adam described it this way: "You sometimes have to be comfortable in not knowing something fully to be able to challenge it. Certain professionals will tell you that you have to do certain things in a linear fashion; otherwise, the world will collapse. Whereas in business, when there is uncertainty, you sometimes just need to think of alternative ways to tackle the problem."

To become comfortable in the unknown is to build your portfolio of experiences so that you are continually learning. The sweet spot for the ambiguity mindset is when you can shift from option to option by challenging assumptions and seeking alternatives, and not get bogged down by the unknowns.

BEHAVIOR PRACTICES

Donald Schön's adaptation of the constructivist viewpoint in the workplace may also provide further insights. Schön argues that employees learn through framing situations through their personal interests and that their knowledge is constructed through reflection during and after the experimental action (Schön, 1983). Gamification and simulations are tools that help executives blend learning. A famous simulation from MIT has stood the test of time in illustrating this point.

EXPLORE UNKNOWNS THROUGH SIMULATION

The Beer Distribution Game was created at MIT by Jay Forrester in 1960 as a simulation of learning from experience. Its purpose is to study managers' decision-making styles during a fictional supply chain process to showcase how ambiguous situations can occur while operating in a

nonunique business model (Forrester, 1971). The original study was conducted with 192 participants and forty-eight trials over four years, and
according to the current MIT News website, the simulation is still being
run in MIT leadership workshops today (Sweeney & Sterman, 2000).

The game consists of groups of four participants representing a bev-
erage retailer, a wholesaler, a distributor, and a brewery. It lasts for fifty
rounds, in which each person faces a decision-making challenge involv-
ing how they manage their current stock inventories and minimize total
costs. Let's use an example of a new craft beer millennials like, which is
trending across cities and creating new customer demand.

The premise of the game is that the retailer receives orders from
customers. There are so many new customers the retailer orders double
the usual weekly order from the wholesaler. The wholesaler sees a pattern of increased orders from other retailers, too, and seeks to fill the
orders but experiences a delivery delay from the distributor. Meanwhile,
the manufacturer is struggling to fill new orders from the various dis-
tributors who submitted increased orders. Challenges occur when each
player must decide how to order from their respective supplier each
week when shipping and receiving experience delays, and the fluctuat-
ing customer demand causes backlogs and increased storage costs.

As the game progresses, there is a continual increase in customer
demand for multiple weeks, after which the demand dissipates. During
the game, even the business students and executives who knew the
intent of the game got sucked into making bad decisions, with at least
one team who quickly lost the supply chain equilibrium and could not
produce enough beer. This shortage resulted in the wholesaler going out
of business, because they had not been given enough craft beer by the
factory and distributor, and the demand dried up.

The Beer Distribution Game shows that operational performance
deteriorates rapidly when more levels of complexity are introduced. In

the experiment, the participants learned weakly and slowly, even with repeated trials, unlimited time, and performance incentives. The game research indicated that heuristics within the game—cookie-cutter responses to unique challenges—produced suboptimal results.

The players were closed in their thinking patterns and failed to take the wider system elements into consideration when making their decisions. This is akin to following management policy (a closed loop) indicators rather than holistic cues from the dynamic external system at large (an open loop) to help make decisions. As one of the players on the losing team said, "We have a strong tendency toward blaming the people for the performance of the system they are in."

Interestingly, the overwhelming learning outcome from the game was that the players learned more from the after-game discussions than from the game itself. This is a huge boost to support lessons-learned activities at corporate workshops. Second, the Beer Distribution Game helped to showcase the external spheres of insight from the organizational and environmental perspective to understand the gray space: people's motivations (to win) as insights and perspectives.

STRATEGIC QUERIES

At any point, the players could have taken a deliberate pause and, as a team, asked a series of questions before the next decision was needed. Similar to those in the competency trap, executives tended to have a tactical give-take relationship with information: When executives need something done, they give directions, and they take information from managers when they need it. The problem is that it is difficult to find a sustainable decision when faced with ambiguous situations with tactical information mechanisms because broader ideas are created through dialogue and collaboration.

Willie Pietersen, author of *Strategic Learning* and professor at Columbia University Business School, claims that the "old, ritualistic, authoritarian methods no longer work today. In a volatile, uncertain, complex and ambiguous (VUCA) environment, our emphasis must shift to insights, ideas and ongoing renewal" (Pietersen, 2010, p. 203).

So let's start by asking the right questions when faced with an unfamiliar situation and avoid falling into the reductionist trap where the thinking becomes deeper and narrows toward one part of a larger system. First, ask, "How does this part (issue) interact with the whole?" Meaning, how does the issue interact with the entire company? This enables you to broaden the scope of the issue into a wider environment and to brainstorm on all the elements that may interact with the issue. For example, the poor sales of the product are not necessarily only a marketing issue.

Second, ask, "What is the behavior of the system?" Consider the following example of how to determine the behavior of the issue: Senior management feels the performance management system is not working well. They think the managers are overrating their direct reports. The managers overrate their direct reports because they think HR places a curve on performance ratings anyway. Senior management already thinks they know who is or is not performing even without seeing the performance ratings.

The behavior of this issue is that the managers start to overrate their employees (a feedback loop) knowing that HR might reduce everyone's rating when it comes time to normalize the ratings (another feedback loop). HR is considering removing the overrating function on the system so the managers cannot use it as the solution to solve the overrating issue (single-loop thinking). Overall, the behavior is a misalignment of the intent of the performance management system.

And the third question is: "How does this part interact with other sections, departments, or products?" Try to explain your understanding of the system you are in as it interacts with other systems. This means you should be able to see the interconnections and interrelationships of all the elements. Try to leverage the three questions with the context to uncover paradoxes and to frame the uniqueness of certain elements to tackle tangled or recurring issues.

IN THE EYE OF THE STORM

You may have noticed that some people thrive in ambiguous situations and seek the eye of the storm. Other seasoned executives who may not have been formally trained in systems thinking or chaos theory have learned to develop this cognitive capacity and are adept at understanding the dynamics that enable good decision-making during uncertain situations. Others recoil at the thought of having to blaze new and unique trails.

Amy, our health care executive, admitted the following: "Some of us gravitate toward ambiguous situations because we like it. I've never been one who liked to have to follow a script. I like being off script. I know using my own critical thinking, coming up with ways of handling things . . . by being in unpredictable situations and seeking all the different things. You do develop intuition based on your experiences."

It just may be your upbringing that allowed you to think forward, as Michael, the hospitality executive, suggested. "I'm sure psychologists would tell you this is significant," he said, laughing. "I am a middle child of a family of five. I had to learn to navigate upward, sideways, and downward. I was always in new situations, as my family moved to a lot of different countries. I jumped multiple grades, which meant that my task was to keep up with the education and also deal with all the people who were more mature than me. There is a certain element of learning to adapt to the unknown."

DIFFERENT SPHERES
OF EXPERIENCES

As was noted in the purposeful research sampling of the twenty-four executives to those who have worked in complex adaptive systems in the UAE, it is logical to conclude that the majority of them would be expatriates. In fact, 92 percent of them were expatriate executives working in the UAE. Additional diversity analysis indicated that 58 percent of the executives had worked in at least three different countries during their career, 41 percent had worked in four different countries, 66 percent spoke a second language, and 41 percent spoke at least three languages. These demographic attributes suggest that the executives may have had experiences in different cultural situations that may have influenced their worldviews and adaptive mental models. Even the executives who were UAE nationals had a global education and international work experiences among a multitude of nationalities, which may have provided a worldview that expanded from the executives' upbringing mental model. The insights into how the executives learned to interact with their social environment through spheres of insight assisted in developing their comfort in the unknown.

During the interviews, 66 percent of the executives described an issue with an operational problem or a large-scale project that required a shift in thinking in order to meet the expected outcomes in which having a dynamic mental model was required. Additionally, 33 percent of them described either an emerging marketing issue (8 percent), innovation (8 percent), or strategic creation (17 percent) as one of the key projects in which a mental model shift was self-evident.

As was noted, the interview transcripts were also analyzed for the number of times the executives explicitly mentioned that a mental model shift took place. The numbers ranged from three to twenty-one, with an average of nine and a half stated mental model shifts mentioned per executive. This data did indicate that each executive was aware of their own cognitive shifts and how the trajectory of their thinking patterns changed based on when they were introduced to new or conflicting information.

You might argue that there is compelling evidence to suggest that the interviewed executives were able to learn how to develop an ambiguity mindset through academic situations; the demographic questionnaire indicated that 75 percent of them have a master's degree, and 58 percent have a master's degree in science or an economic-based field, such as economics, information management and systems, nursing, or industrial engineering, where systems or complexity theory may have been part of the curriculum. However, the executives referred only a few times to their academic history during the interviews, and those were in the context of their understanding of events within the university experience rather than any specific curriculum-based learning moments.

The majority of the executives' excerpts claimed they learned from situations, their social circle, and the changing environment. Given the context of the narratives, it appears that they learned informally (per Marsick and Watkins's [2001] informal and incidental learning theory); that they learned within nonroutine conditions; or that critical reflection was used to clarify a situation. In a plethora of stories, the executives described their learning experiences through unique and complex situations that were part of their everyday encounters, working within complex adaptive systems or even before their professional careers were established.

Learning from experience was part of the journey. Three of the executives I interviewed described poignant distressing or unique situations in their upbringing that enabled them to learn early in life that their points of reference (or cognitive navigation) required a conscious understanding of the situation. This was manifested in the executives' narratives and their approach to understanding ambiguity and uncertain situations. Their previous experiences provided them with knowledge and confidence that suspending judgment, seeking perspectives, and taking the time to pause, reflect, and think through the next potential step with collaborative discussions and critical dialogue would facilitate a positive result.

Furthermore, the narratives from the social, cultural, and community practices were strong influencers. This indicated that the executives' learned experiences were highly contextual.

TYPES OF VALUABLE LEARNING EXPERIENCES

Three types of experiences were prevalent from the narratives in the executives' interviews: ambiguous situations, exposure to alternative ways of thinking, and challenging assumptions.

AMBIGUOUS SITUATIONS

The executives elicited valuable lessons from being immersed in uncertain situations that may not have occurred in routine circumstances, and they paid attention to their own learning from the experience.

For example, renewable energy executive Charlie used the analogy of an unknown forest: "When I get into these ambiguous and conflict situations, that's when I learned that I'm in a spot where value can happen. I feel like I'm trekking in an unknown forest looking for a big waterfall somewhere. I learned to be very curious. I get very focused, and you look for handholds in this landscape or whatever metaphors to create my path through it."

On the other hand, Michael, the hospitality executive, learned that collaboration with employees can untangle complex issues; more importantly, he doesn't believe a complex situation is a barrier. "Once you involve people in solving really complex issues, which a number of people don't think we'd ever be able to find a solution, it becomes contagious. It becomes a way of life. You know, I can do it, and there's no saying no to this unique situation."

Although managing the unexpected is necessary in complex adaptive systems, learning to develop an ambiguity mindset can include a scan of the senses. Amy, the health care executive, explained, "I am absorbing color, taste, touch, and using all my senses to size up the unique situation. By being in unpredictable situations and seeing all the different things, you do develop intuition based on your experiences."

The rewards of being involved in dynamic and unique systems can contribute to deeper learning. Shipping executive Marcus's narrative mirrored that premise. He mentioned a new project with limited resources in an uncertain environment. "The project was almost impossible to deliver. It was two years of hardships—a lot of stress; 24/7 working; I had no social life, but it was really rewarding, because I discovered a lot of new ways to find solutions to problems."

EXPOSURE TO ALTERNATIVE WAYS OF THINKING

All the executive narratives pointed toward having exposure to alternative ways of thinking as an influence on developing an ambiguity mindset. However, in this area, they cited more diverse experiences. For example, 42 percent of the responses pointed toward team discussion as being an important element for finding an alternative way to think, with 8 percent stating specifically that diverse voices on the team are valuable. Seventeen percent of the executives cited meeting thought leaders or reading business or leadership books as helping them develop alternative ways of thinking. This included the education executive, Daniel, who stated, "My life changed when I read *Men Are from Mars, Women Are from Venus*. I was a teenager when I read it, but I began to understand a different language. It helped me to decode perspectives. And the book *Thinking, Fast and Slow* by Daniel Kahneman and his phrase 'What you see is all there is' struck me."

Similarly, Adam, our real estate executive, explained, "I remember early in my career thinking that this new project was so complicated, and then I saw someone think through it so easily. He was a senior person that I worked with, and he literally did an entire feasibility study of a new project on a Post-it note. It turns out that you can do that, if you have enough experiences in different contexts, if you are listening, and if you pick up what is happening. Now after all these years, I realize that it wasn't so complicated; I just learned how to think with that mindset."

Other executives cited mentors (8 percent), cultural experiences (17 percent), and executive coaching (17 percent) as important influencers. Stepping outside of your individual sphere and into the organizational and environmental spheres helps provide the learning experiences to develop an ambiguity mindset.

CHALLENGING ASSUMPTIONS

All the executives provided an example of how they learned to challenge their own assumptions or the situation to find good learning moments. Challenging personal, behavioral, or organizational assumptions is also part of an adaptable mental model. Health care executive Amy described a process to challenge assumptions. "You see something highly unusual, or you'll see something that deserves attention, deconstruction, root cause analysis, or other, so you can figure out why it happened like that. Much of the time, what you think caused the problem is not what caused it, and you don't know that until you really ask a lot of questions and do a lot of digging to find that out."

Charlie, our renewable energy executive, posited that value is created when the status quo is questioned. "You are diving into processes, and suddenly, you become self-involved. You become the process, the governance of your world of perspectives. Therefore, you lose perspective; you lose sight of opportunities. If you don't reflect that, are you doing the right work?"

Adam, the real estate executive, stated, "I try to use humor. I'm trying to make light of the situation, explain it, or articulate it to someone else. The point is to explain the absurdity of something in a different form, because when you are embarking on something unknown and people don't understand, you sometimes need to approach it or translate it totally different for others to get it."

Other executives spoke to their own assumptions being challenged, which provided learning insights. The information and technology executive, Karim, stated that a thought leader's business course on strategic advocacy helped him understand the holistic nature of seeking different perspectives for good business outcomes. Karim said, "I loved this model of strategic advocacy taught at Columbia University, because it opens your eyes as to how other stakeholders are positioned vis-à-vis your advocacy, and to what you can do in order to bring them closer to your line of thinking. This is an 'aha!' learning after thirty years as a professional."

Reflect back on Robert from the IT department. Receiving simplistic feedback that he was not acting as an effective leader and then being subsequently challenged by senior management to perform better was a telling learning moment. Interestingly, sometimes it is the humble learning moments—the harsh message, the alternative viewpoint, the realization that things are not working—that create the impetus for a thinking change. Seeking out those critical but supportive voices is valuable.

In the course of interviewing the executives, I collected data regarding all the experiences the executives mentioned. The data analysis showed the type of experiences the executives described during the interviews and the frequency of those experiences. Table 1 illustrates that the top five types of experiences equated to 68 percent of all the experiences referenced: perspective taking, a situation related to one's upbringing, socioeconomic forces, sharing knowledge, and humble leadership moments. And the top three types of experiences equated to 48 percent of all the experiences mentioned: perspective taking, a situation related to one's upbringing, and socioeconomic forces.

Table 1. Narratives of types of experiences and frequency

TYPE OF EXPERIENCE	FREQUENCY
Perspective taking	12
Situation related to one's upbringing	8
Socioeconomic forces	8
Sharing knowledge	7
Humble leadership moments	6
Puzzling moments	5
Career choice	3
Information seeking	2
Workplace inefficiencies	2
Strategic dilemma	2
Learning about behaviors	2
Big-picture understanding	1
Corporate community building	1
Office politics	1
Total	60

The wide range of experiences cited in the narratives points toward a wide view of the personal, organizational, and environmental spheres in terms of learning cues to build an ambiguity mindset, with fourteen different types of learning experiences identified. Furthermore, 91 percent were informal learning experiences, outside of a formal learning environment, reinforcing the idea that an ambiguity mindset is not a classroom-learned skill.

In conjunction, Table 2 shows the type of experiences expressed in the salient narratives for the research question: What experiences and events provide the scaffolding in developing an ambiguity mindset? The responses indicated a variety of experiences that span the three spheres of insight: individual, organizational, and environmental. Specifically, 43 percent of the first research question responses aligned with internal or individual cognitive learning experiences, which placed emphasis

Table 2. Types of experiences within spheres of insight

SPHERE OF INSIGHT	TYPE OF EXPERIENCE	PERCENTAGE OF EXPERIENCES IN THIS SPHERE
Environment	Upbringing Socioeconomic forces Big-picture understanding	21
Individual	Taking perspective Humble leadership moments Puzzling moments Career choice Information sharing Learning about behaviors	43
Organizational	Sharing knowledge Workplace inefficiencies Strategic dilemma Corporate community building Office politics	36

on reflective learning and adaptive mental models techniques, while 36 percent of the responses were within the context of organizational learning moments, and 21 percent of the responses were in relation to the executive's environment, whether that meant an event associated with their upbringing, paying attention to the big picture, or various socioeconomic forces.

What does all this analysis mean? It means that the role of ambiguous experiences is paramount for developing comfort in the unknown and developing a strategic learning path. Similar to how you must read a recipe to learn to cook, you must also get on the bike to feel, see, and create a sense of balance to learn to ride a bike. Our esteemed and humble executives detailed stories of how they embraced the messy and noisy experiences and events in order to learn how to navigate future disconnects, weak signals, misguided agendas, and paradoxes. The executives detailed three actions that helped build their ambiguity mindset: seeking ambiguous situations, being exposed to alternative ways of thinking, and experiencing challenging situations by paying attention to all three spheres of insight (individual, organizational, and environmental).

Key Takeaways

Find ambiguous situations. Learning through tough situations is a humbling experience. But how do you learn through these unique situations if you are not an expatriate living and working overseas? Or if you are stuck in a routine job and nothing new ever happens? Or if you tend to back away from new experiences? You start small. You join a new club where you don't know people. Learn an activity in which you have no experience, or volunteer for the next work project. By being open to new experiences and remaining humble as you embrace them, you will learn from other people, situations, and the environment and will start to build the ambiguity mindset.

Challenge assumptions. As an executive, you should be focused on how to expand the team's cognitive processes in the workplace and provide your teams with new duties, new responsibilities, and a culturally diverse environment. You might also provide stretch projects to develop the ambiguity thinking and learning opportunities to build the incremental cognitive strength muscles. As an executive, you should understand this adult learning concept to ensure that everyone, from all levels within the company, seeks meaning from informal learning events.

Expose yourself to alternative ways of thinking. Seek out people who you know don't think like you. Embrace different expertise from a variety of domains, not only to explore how others might view an issue but also to understand how they collaborate, share knowledge and workplace processes, and discuss different points of view. By expanding your comfort zone into all three spheres of insight, you are able to seek more evidence and scrutinize the best decision pathway.

. . . . .

CHAPTER 4

LEARN THROUGH PERSON, CONTEXT, AND ENVIRONMENT

Kurt Lewin, a German American psychologist from the early 1900s, is recognized as the founder of social psychology and was instrumental in deepening our understanding of action research and group dynamics. Lewin suggested that neither nature nor nurture shapes an individual; rather, it is the interaction of both. He was famous for his formula $B = f(P, E)$, which means that an individual's behavior (B) is a function (f) of the interactions between the person (P) and the environment (E) (Lewin, 1936). Simply stated, your behavior can be determined by your situation, and your behavior is different depending on the tension between your perceptions of yourself and the environment.

Bill Pasmore, author of *Advanced Consulting*, states that this formula explains why some people can react differently during an organizational change project or when a company installs a new reward system—the environment is changing, and you should expect changes in the employees' behavior (Pasmore, 2020). Pasmore further states that "when coaching an executive, it is not easy to change who they are—the (P), but in a different environment (E), the executive can easily experiment with different ways of behaving. And that's exactly what many leadership development programs do—they provide executives with opportunities to try out new behaviors in a safe setting instead of on the job" (Pasmore, 2020, p. 125).

Dr. Caridad Vivian Chrisomalis conducted a qualitative study with nine executive coaches to shed light on the factors perceived to influence the transformation of their mindsets (fixed or growth mindset) with the potential for enhanced *feedback receptivity*—which is a skill perceived to enhance an executive coach's ability to coach clients. Chrisomalis was seeking to examine the factors that affect the coaching program and verify if the program is effective for a leadership behavior change. One element of the study was to overlay Lewin's theory $B = f(P, E)$ by feedback receptivity (B) = the interplay (f) between two self-focused factors (i.e., mindset and feedback orientation) (P) and two context-focused factors (feedback environment and learning climate) (E).

Through a series of feedback methods, the study revealed the link between an individual's mindset, feedback orientation, and the feedback environment. The study also confirmed that psychological safety and professional development—the environment (E)—enables a good learning climate and has a positive impact on the coaches' ability to coach (Chrisomalis, 2021).

What does this mean for learning how to develop an ambiguity mindset? When you are immersed in uncertain environments, you need to increase understanding of everyone's context and environment. While it is typical to focus on the *person* we see in the office environment, it is more difficult to understand or see the person's behavior in different environments. A multifaced and multidimensional view is needed. This is no easy feat. Think about all the relevant details about yourself that shape your behavior, identity, belief system, and values. Or how you make decisions based on your experiences, knowledge, and expertise. Or how your behavior is also shaped by your environment, culture, social institutions, family, community groups, and other social movements. So when stuck in unfamiliar situations, you must also try to understand other people's behaviors, context, and environment and use myriad ways to seek clarity on the continual changing of dynamic concepts to even begin to predict someone's behavior for the next uncertain step.

ORCHESTRA OF BALANCE

On August 5, 2010, over seven hundred thousand tons of rock collapsed into the Chilean San Jose mine, trapping thirty-three miners seven hundred meters below the surface. Over the course of sixty-nine days, there was massive confusion and misinformation among the mine owners, the government, the Chilean mining community, and the geology drilling companies. The barriers to rescue the miners seemed insurmountable; the mine had long, sloping tunnels that sprawled sixteen kilometers underground, it was missing escape ladders in the ventilation shafts, they could find only outdated maps, and there were no backup exits. A massive rock, which was twice as hard as granite, had blocked the mine entrance. As the rescue progressed, six drilling spots were identified as areas where oxygen and supplies could be transported to the spots where experts thought the miners were located.

A command post was set up, communication and technical teams were created, and drilling started. But the challenges were unique: The available drill bits had a 5 percent precision range, meaning that drilling at a depth of seven hundred meters, they could miss the miners' identified locations by meters.

Global experts began arriving in San Jose and conducted daily meetings with the decision makers to verify whether new or faster drilling technology was available. Experts from 3D software drilling companies, geologists, and health and safety companies presented alternative solutions. Even NASA provided recommendations on the mental health issues that might arise among the miners during prolonged periods of stress, confinement to a small space, and fatigue.

Meanwhile, medical professionals began advising the miners below ground of the rescue operation, which would include rescue capsules that were to be pulled through the drilled hole. As the world watched, on the sixty-ninth day, all the Chilean miners were pulled through the capsule tunnel and rescued (Rashid, Edmondson, Leonard, 2013).

Amy Edmondson and Jean-Francois Harvey wrote about the incident in their book *Extreme Teaming: Lessons in Complex, Cross-Sector Leadership*. The experts, they say, thought the rescue would be impossible, because the issues spanned across physical, organizational, cultural, geographic, and professional boundaries. Ultimately, however, the rescue resulted in a positive outcome from a concept they call *extreme teaming*. The authors describe the complex system of the mine collapse and the mindsets of the leaders, technicians, internal consultants, rescued miners, and media as a balanced orchestra of leaders constantly "exploring, experimenting, and inventing together and integrating deep knowledge and ideas—not just applying them" (Edmondson & Harvey, 2017, p. 111).

The disaster exemplified how, during times of stress, it is imperative to step outside of your own mindset, to build situation awareness, to tap into the expertise of others, and to gain a wide-angle lens to expand your worldview. While you might not ever become involved in a scenario such as the Chilean mine or the 2018 Thailand cave incident where a group of boys went exploring and ended up trapped deep inside a cave underneath a mountain, there are many people who have been involved in civil strife or experienced extreme confusion regarding social injustices. And everyone has had their life changed in some manner by the COVID-19 pandemic.

Your ability to understand the individual, organizational, and environmental spheres of insight, with insights into people, their context, and their environment, to understand unique situations with more clarity will enable you to be better able to make informed choices.

SOCIAL INTELLIGENCE

Knowledge work is increasingly important, as the remote workplace is becoming more mainstream and new processes are needed to keep people linked to the business. The ambiguity game is about tapping into the richness of the individual, organizational, and environmental spheres with all the dynamic changes that occur within each sphere. The focus is not only on how to expand your own mental models but also on how to pay attention to the mindsets of those in your social systems to enhance the quality of your thinking.

The paradox is that to lead, you must relinquish power and create an environment that taps into the social intelligence, the capacity to know oneself and others. Social intelligence is developed by learning from everyone's experiences, seeking to understand cultural and personal differences, and listening with an open mind.

The executive interviews revealed a strong link to the social constructivist lens, which encompasses the social and cultural environments of how the executives can build their cognitive intellectual capacity by understanding the person, the environment, and the social forces that may act on them.

Michael, the hospitality executive, said, "I will take the time and speak to all people who work for the company. So, whether they are a security guard or a janitor, or a managing director, every job's important, so every individual is important. If you start from that perspective, then you'll take time to listen to people, and you'll be able to rally people to do the extraordinary." Social intelligence helps explain the types of perspectives required to attain a holistic social constructivist worldview that leads to an ambiguity mindset.

The focus on discovering intelligence from the person, context, and environment helps us understand the link between social psychology and the hard-to-predict influences on behavior. It shows how becoming more aware of social cues; understanding your team's background, upbringing, and education; and learning how their lived experiences can play a strong role in their assumptions and biases within the workplace are crucial for addressing ambiguity. Connecting into this network is taking a deep dive into the other person's social cognition and their socioeconomic or political challenges to understand the interconnections among the person, the context, and the environment to begin to influence, guide, and explore the invisible dynamics of the workplace.

LEARNING AGILITY

Regardless of who you are or how high up the corporate ladder you are, one of the biggest barriers to decoding principles of the ambiguity mindset is not the lack of time, resources, or cognitive power; it may be your lack of motivation to learn something new. When conducting leadership workshops with the senior teams, facilitators must always brace themselves for the "I already know that" statements or for the obvious displeasure the executives express at being in a room where they are expected to learn. As Leonardo, the private equity executive, put it, "The biggest risk is to go into a formal fossilization. You get pushed by a series of events into a comfort zone with which, over time, you grow complacent, and then you're unable to get out of it. This is particularly dangerous if you are a CEO."

As an executive, you may assume that you already know and use the skills you're purportedly learning, or your pride, self-doubt, or ego may distort your own self-importance. Either way, there is a way to check yourself and to ensure that you embrace the time and effort needed to learn the nuances of people, context, and environment, and their inter-relationships in the workplace. This is done by learning more about the concept of learning agility.

Dr. W. Warner Burke, an Edward Lee Thorndike professor of psychology and education at Teachers College, Columbia University, has written more than one hundred articles on organizational psychology and leadership development, as well as many articles on the concept of learning agility. *Learning agility* can be defined as a combination of motivation—being willing to face new and perhaps ambiguous situations by taking actions that help you stay engaged—and the skills to discern quickly the consequences of these actions, determining what to do next to continue the process of learning (Burke et al., 2016, p. 2). Essentially, learning agility has two components: learning a set of skills and being motivated. Burke also says that your willingness to take risks in ambiguous new situations acts as feedback about your performance.

When was the last time you asked for performance feedback? Burke jokes during a *Talks at Columbia* presentation at Columbia University that you can't be an agile learner if you don't ask for feedback because of the risk, of course, that you might actually get feedback you don't want to hear. But this is precisely the skill that is needed to be an agile learner. Based on Burke's (2017) measurement of learning agility, the nine learning agility determinants are these:

- Flexibility: being open to new ideas and proposing new solutions

- Speed: acting on ideas quickly so that those not working are discarded and other possibilities accelerated

- Experimenting: trying new behaviors, approaches, or ideas to determine what is effective

- Performance risk taking: seeking new activities—tasks, assignments, roles—that provide opportunities to be challenged

- Interpersonal risk taking: discussing differences with others in ways that lead to learning and change

- Collaborating: finding new ways to work with others that generate new opportunities for learning

- Information gathering: using various methods to remain current in your area of expertise

- Feedback seeking: asking others for feedback on your ideas and overall performance

- Reflecting: slowing down to evaluate your own performance to be more effective

The elements of learning agility are both cognitive and behavioral; leaders are continually developing, growing, and using new ways of thinking and behavior strategies that involve knowing others' context and environment better in order to be better able to face uncertainty in the workplace.

The executives I interviewed also exemplified learning in their narratives. This was evident when Karim, the information and technology executive, stated, "When you are operating in emerging markets, you find yourself addressing a large spectrum of problems and challenges. You have to think constantly about what motivates others, what is their learning process, how to best communicate with them, and how to effectively advocate your position. And you're doing all of that in an environment that is moving rapidly. There is no room for static thinking here."

The executives described their challenges and how they learned their ambiguity mindset, which blended insights from the three spheres of insight. Oil and gas executive Rachid explained how the different personalities and diversity of his team enhanced their strategic outputs, provided insights that helped build organizational capacity, and were influenced by economic factors. Furthermore, the shipping executive, Marcus, described the social, cultural, and community practices as strong influencers on the company's success.

SOFT POWER FOR CORPORATE VALUE

Adult learning theories are intrinsically linked to creating corporate value and the strategic and financial targets. To not address these soft power issues is to invite knowing gaps into your business. Executive thinking is focused primarily on the strategic and financial targets for the company, and it is common for executives to just want the employees to do their jobs. The executives may disregard concepts such as employee motivation, engagement, and psychological safety. However, forward-thinking executives recognize that an employee-centered approach yields untapped value.

For example, Herbert C. Kelman, professor of social ethics at Harvard University, provides a framework in his social influence theory to explore how an employee's emotions, opinions, and behaviors are affected by others (Kelman, 1958). If negativity is prevalent in the workplace, it can spread throughout the company. Small, unexpected negative events can have a ripple effect throughout the organization and can potentially cause disproportional consequences or recurring issues. Additionally, the complexity leadership theory offers leadership behavioral insights into complex adaptive systems, positing that "relationships are no longer hierarchical but rather interactions and contain heterogeneous agents and work across agent networks" (Lichtenstein et al., 2006, p. 2).

Wilfred H. Drath, senior fellow from the Center for Creative Leadership, contends that "people construct reality through their interactions within worldviews. They do it when they explain things to one another, tell each other stories, create models and theories, and when they generally interact through thought, work, and action" (Drath, 2001, p. 136). The corporate strategy may be a comprehensive document that outlines all the projects the company seeks to achieve; however, it is the people that make the strategy come to fruition. This is the time-consuming organizational behavior ethos in which, if you want your strategy to succeed, you will need to invest the time to understand the people, context, and environment.

MIND MAPPING

Another valuable ambiguity mindset development tool is the cause-effect mind mapping exercise. Mind maps represent your train of thought on a given topic. The premise is to illustrate the relationships between ideas and concepts and to show how they connect with one another.

I conducted a focus group exercise with a different group of executives who thrive in complex adaptive systems to examine the cause-effect relationship of ambiguity within the workplace, to explore how the executives learned this skill, and to discover their perceptions or beliefs of the unexpected errors that occurred at work. I started the exercise by asking the executives to choose a past ambiguous situation in the workplace that had a negative outcome (i.e., the outcome did not meet their expectations). They were asked to draw the central idea in the middle of the page. Then, the executives were asked to identify the main primary ideas that emanated directly from the central idea and to include words that best described the situation, event, or person (these are nodes). The next step for them was to identify the connection of the secondary ideas that occurred in the past project.

Next, I asked the group to take a different colored pen and identify the connections—the lessons learned—in terms of cause and effect. For example, because of a lack of stakeholder communication with one vendor, the vendor refused to sign a document, which delayed the project for two weeks. In other words, the executives needed to identify the surprises that occurred within the project scope. They also needed to highlight the additional links and interactions that occurred during the project that were not planned. And finally, the group was asked to highlight the connections to the primary and secondary ideas that had a positive or negative feedback loop, as demonstrated in Figure 7.

Through the discussion and activity, the original number of perceived relationships more than doubled once the executives began to see the hidden relationships and connections that caused issues to arise. Interestingly, they mentioned they had forgotten about some conflicting issues that occurred within the project until they started drawing the mind map—issues that could have caused future errors in new projects.

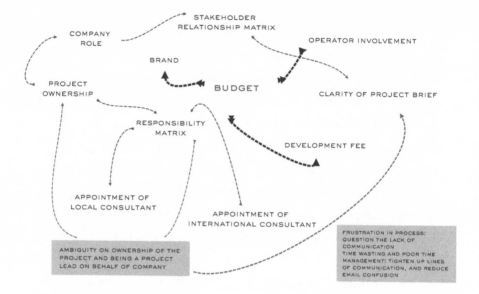

FIGURE 7. CAUSE-EFFECT AMBIGUITY MIND MAP

The mind map exercise included identifying the interrelationships, the negative and positive feedback loops, the unknown or ambiguous elements, and the cause-effect relationships with the event. Within each causal map, there was an average of ten nodes for each scenario, an average of fifteen nonlinear interactions and relationships between the elements, and an average of five positive and negative feedback loops linked to cause-and-effect variables. Systems thinking experts claim that, within organizations, the higher the number of interactions (people's behaviors, beliefs, and attitudes) within the system, the harder it is to predict the system's behavior.

After the mind maps were completed, I posed five questions to the executives. The first was "How do you try to understand ambiguity?" Through the multiple responses provided, everyone in the focus group stated that understanding the different perspectives was important; they included statements such as "I try to understand the true motivation of decision makers" and "I try to understand the people and their drivers."

The top three responses were as follows: 66 percent of the group listed communication as important, while 32 percent tried to collect information (in a variety of forms), and 32 percent of the group stated that reflection was a way to try to understand ambiguity.

The second question was "What are your perceptions of or beliefs about the unexpected changes (cause-effect)?" The top three responses were as follows: 83 percent of the group answered with operational structure issues (unqualified decision makers, a need for clear roles and responsibilities, and a lack of time), whereas 66 percent added that a lack of understanding others' behavior can lead to errors, and 32 percent of the group stated that the level of complexity and the elements involved are variables of unexpected changes.

The third question was "When you are faced with a puzzling pattern of events, what significant learning moments helped you to understand?" The top four responses included 50 percent of the group, who stated that previous complex experiences were helpful; 50 percent, who thought that cultural experiences were important; 32 percent of the group, who cited their MBA experiential experiences as insights—specifically when during project work, they learned how teams with equally smart people can function totally differently—and 50 percent of the group, who stated that they consult mentors or trusted or knowledgeable friends to gain a better understanding of uncertain events.

The fourth question was "When you have a good ambiguity learning moment, what elements, people, or influencers are present?" The top three responses were as follows: 83 percent of the group stated that having a colleague with a forward-thinking mindset was beneficial, 32 percent said they had access to contextual information to gain more understanding, and 16 percent of the group raised intuition as important. As one of the executives noted, "You need to be able to sense the change coming."

The final question was "If you were to guide future leaders through ambiguous situations, what thinking strategies would you use?" The top three responses were that half the focus group indicated that they would need to understand the true nature of the projects and would try to seek agenda alignment with others before the project began, 32 percent of the group stated that multiple thinking styles were important to see the different elements of the ambiguity that might not be apparent, and 16 percent pointed to building a network as important. As one of the executives said after the exercise in a reflective tone, "I guess what I have learned is that, if you are surprised by someone's behavior in the workplace, you just have not been paying attention."

Chris Argyris's research addresses organizational issues, and he analyzed over one thousand interview transcripts of people who participated in a study. The results show that the executives made inferences about another person's behavior without checking whether those inferences were valid, and they advocated their own views abstractly without explaining or illustrating their reasons (Argyris, 1980).

To promote better business outcomes, you need only look to some of the costly incidents that have occurred with big corporations to see the causes and effects of a poor understanding of employees' behaviors. For example, Uber stated in 2019, when faced with public sexual harassment and gender discrimination charges, "Our workplace culture and forward-leaning approach created significant operational and cultural challenges that have in the past harmed, and may in the future continue to harm, our business results and financial condition. [Uber's] focus on aggressive growth and intense competition . . . [created] a lack of transparency [and resulted in] siloed teams that lack coordination and knowledge sharing" (Wong, 2019).

Knowing that problems are abundant and that other people's perceptions are your reality, along with understanding more about other people's own assumptions and biases, may help you gain greater efficiency and new perspectives on how to understand ambiguous situations before they appear on the news.

ORGANIZATIONAL LEARNING

The ability to leverage corporate intelligence is paramount to corporate competitiveness and sustainability and is especially important during times of change and uncertainty. The book *If Only We Knew What We Know: The Transfer of Internal Knowledge and Best Practice* speaks to how organizational learning and leveraging knowledge-sharing programs is an underused strategic intent (O'Dell & Grayson, 1998).

Organizational learning plays an important role within the adult learning theories, because the workplace is an important knowledge-sharing location. Michael Eraut, the UK's leading researcher on how professionals learn in workplace settings, states, "Knowledge of context and organizations is often acquired through a process of socialization through observation, induction, and increasing participation rather than formal inquire" (Eraut, 2000, p. 122). Organizational learning expands from an individual perspective and builds the idea of a network of knowledge, while employees are seen as the individual agents empowered to learn from their environments.

Knowledge is hidden in the workplace and is often hard to harness; therefore, the underused concept of organizational learning can help. It is difficult to ensure that people share knowledge in their areas, so companies can take advantage of what they already know. Holland argued that complexity increases for learning within complex adaptive systems, because the conditional interactions play such an important role (Holland, 2005). As hospitality executive Michael put it, "You have to understand the different drivers because it is not always clear at first sight. And so, you find yourself spending more and more time trying to understand what drives people."

Marcus, the shipping executive, said, "Because every senior executive or general manager has to make that transition away from 'I'm an expert' and 'I'm going to tell everybody what to do,' which limits your capability, ability, and horsepower, and you must engage with people on a more personal level."

Even simple mechanisms with simple interactions can generate complex behaviors. This leads to the notion that an ambiguity mindset and organizational learning are interrelated as continual learning and awareness of knowledge gaps. Peter Senge says, "Organizations learn only through individuals who learn" (Senge, 1990, p. 129).

Organizational learning can be accomplished by becoming more disciplined in understanding the premise of knowledge, how it is created, and how it can become a form of competitive advantage. This focus helped to revolutionize how workplace learning occurs. Previously, workplace learning was thought of as a training event; however, the principles of organizational learning, as Peter Senge (1990) puts it, are more about how to create ideas, move the ideas across the organization to create new knowledge, and respond to the environment accordingly. Because of the incredibly fast pace of corporate change owing to technological advancements, workplace learning should be the strategic business modus operandi.

Learning is gained by creating widespread mechanisms to tap into the value of social situations and interactions and to adopt corporate learning opportunities from informal learning situations—how people interact, promote dialogue, or share information. Marcus reflected on new and uncertain situations with organizational learning techniques in this way: "Well, I think if you are an executive here [in the UAE] or somewhere else in the world where you're not necessarily from, it's a guarantee that you're going to have to spend a lot more time on things that don't directly relate to your business, but it has to do with being able to get inside and understand what's going on around you. If you don't understand it, you can't anticipate it; then everything will be unexpected."

Charlie, the renewable energy executive, pointed to people who are authentic. "I'm looking for authenticity to help me navigate. If you can find authentic people providing authentic information, that's a double confirmation. It is the people-driven approach, and I've learned after a while, because I used to draw myself into the numbers and ask people for more numbers. It turns out that if you're just numbers driven, then you're only going to get as far as the mathematics can show you. If you are people driven, then you can actually discover new territory."

When working in new situations or with diverse groups of people, the technical knowledge or expertise in your domain is important, but learning through interactions with others and understanding their behaviors and attitudes are equally—if not more—important. This is where the fluid and dynamic changes can occur and where they need to be absorbed.

CULTURE RICH

There are reams of research studies showcasing that cultural diversity positively affects board decisions and creates more effective teams. Katherine W. Phillips, Columbia Business School professor and author of *How Diversity Makes Us Smarter*, states that "being around people who are different from us makes us more creative, more diligent and harder-working" (Phillips, 2014). While research has also shown that diversity of race, ethnicity, gender, and sexual orientation can cause workplace discomfort, rougher interactions, or a lack of trust, the upside is that if you want to build teams to innovate, the diversity enhances creativity and can improve the bottom line of companies (Phillips, 2014). This is the strategic link that will help you cultivate diverse views, mindsets, and experiences. Immersing yourself in different situations to learn from others of different cultures and backgrounds is a crucial part of the ambiguity mindset.

The following executive excerpts point toward adaptive responses as they unfold for meaning making in certain types of community or cultural situations. Marcus, the shipping executive, detailed a unique work experience in which he didn't understand why the workers failed to respect work attendance rules. He found that the regular business practices of warning letters or disciplinary action were not effective.

Knowing that the workforce was mainly foreign nationals, Marcus needed to better understand their culture and customs. He said, "I couldn't get my arms around the attendance issue, with lots of people from Yemen, Oman, India, and the Philippines, and what I found out is that if 20 percent of the workforce does not show up, it has something to do with a celebration or something. And you know, that's when you get into learning about certain values, systems. And so I looked at getting advice and visited the sheikh of those tribes. I found out that there are all these different structures in the way societies are managed. If you don't want to understand it, you are going to have an issue, so you have to adjust."

Transportation executive Luc also described the importance of international relations: "Well, most things in life are not linear. You just try to see what the other side is trying to achieve. In certain societies, that is a lot easier. If I'm talking to a European—German or Swiss—banker, it's very easy. They don't beat around the bush. If you are having the same conversation in environments like the UAE, Saudi Arabia, or Egypt, what the other person is telling you sometimes has five different meanings. You have to be able to read between the lines. This is the most difficult thing to do." David, our academic executive, was equally focused on seeking alternative ways of thinking and said, "I didn't have a mentor per se. But I found a group of people that had many experiences that I could tap into. I learned from the collective."

Paying attention to the thinking and behavior patterns, specifically for people with different or unique views, is important. You need to be open to learning through the interactions and must develop the ability to take cues from the context and integrate them into a new situation. As the academic executive, David, stated, "That was a stunner to me. I was in a whole different culture: in this case, the UAE—and now, reflecting, I didn't get it. I didn't understand how these people work, the politics of it. It was some rough roads, and I got used to it, and I adapted. Part of the adapting was learning how structurally things work, how decisions are made, also what autonomy that you have. I learned through experience."

The mantra of learning from different people, contexts, and environments was manifested in the executives' narratives and their approach to understanding ambiguous situations. Their previous experiences had provided them with the knowledge and confidence that suspending judgment, seeking perspectives, and taking the time to pause, reflect, and think through the next potential step with collaborative discussions and critical dialogue would facilitate a positive result.

The interviewed executives are of the notion that seeking to control elements (agents) within complex adaptive systems is futile. They realized that the systems they're working in can change and can be changed by influencing the various behaviors and thinking patterns of the people involved (including them).

Amy, our health care executive, said, "Not the whole time but much of the time, I was the only female on the team. I've learned that diversity is really important. I have been an advocate to have additional diversity on the team." Michael, the hospitality executive, similarly stated, "You need to ensure you don't employ look-alikes. You need to have a mixture of different people, to bring different personalities together, because different situations will need different skills." By learning more about the cultural differences, you are able to navigate through different contexts more effectively.

Dr. Linda Gironda, an attorney and college educator in New York, conducted research to explore how adult educators use a blended teaching format to promote cross-cultural understanding between students from different cultures. Her research examined how universities use online technology to connect students from different countries to work in cross-cultural teams as a way to develop intercultural competence, promote diversity, and challenge stereotypes (Gironda, 2019).

One of the findings, the power of paradox of synchronicity, examined the power distance across cultures and within cultures. The results appeared to show the educators from the United States had greater authority over those from Mexico when it came to dictating the class schedule, and both groups willingly accepted this uneven distribution of power. The research, however, revealed another type of power distance—that is, within cultures. In Mexico, the adult educators had greater power over their students to change the schedule and demand that students attend class outside the regular schedule. In the United States, adult educators stated that they simply did not have that level of authority over their students and were bound by the committed class schedule. The research revealed a paradox of power: While the US instructors appeared to have power across cultures, it was really Mexican instructors who had greater power within their culture to achieve the goal of cross-cultural understanding (Gironda, 2019).

Finding people in the organization who embody the ability to seek

understanding and learn from cultural diversity can enhance the different teams' deliverables.

ILLUMINATING DIFFERENCES FOR UNDERSTANDING

Consider *the dress*, the 2015 internet viral sensation. Millions of people
were divided on the color of a dress. A lady from Scotland posted a
photo on Facebook of a dress that she wanted to wear to her friend's
wedding to gain feedback from her family and friends. From the posted
comments, you could see there was something interesting going on;
there was a plethora of conflicting posted comments about whether the
dress was black and blue or gold and white. The topic soon caught the
attention of cognitive science researchers.

Around the world, people saw two different color combinations.
Some saw the dress color as gold and white (something you should
not wear to a wedding), and others saw black and blue (which is the
original color of the dress if you were to be face-to-face with the dress).
Researchers were keen to jump into this polarizing disagreement. Very
quickly, the researchers determined that the differing color perspectives
were not owing to varying computer screens. They also found that one
group couldn't be convinced of the other group's color combination.

New York University neuroscientist Pascal Wallisch created a study
with more than thirteen thousand participants to find out whether the
differences of opinion were based on gender, geographical location,
age, or other factors. What Wallisch and his team concluded from the
research was that these differences in perception were due to how the
dress was lit (Wallisch, 2017). The dress was originally photographed in
a shop dressing room and illuminated by artificial light.

In the study, published in the *Journal of Vision*, Wallisch's team asked the participants to verify whether they viewed the dress as being in a shadow or not. Among those who saw it as a shadow, four of five participants—80 percent—believed the dress to be white and gold; by contrast, only about half—50 percent—of the participants who did not see it as being in a shadow saw the garment as black and blue. Wallisch then asked the participants whether they go to bed early and feel at their best in the morning; these were classified as *larks*. If the participant instead liked to sleep in and felt best at night, they were classified as *owls*. Wallisch then matched the participants' self-identified circadian type with the colors they saw in the dress (Wallisch, 2017).

He hypothesized that the different perceptions were linked to the subjects' exposure to daylight. Quite simply, the larks—the people who rise early, go to bed early, and spend many of their waking hours in sunlight—were more likely to see the dress as white and gold than were the owls, whose world is illuminated not by the sun but, rather, by wavelengths of artificial light and who would see the dress as black and blue. Wallisch explained, "The original dress image was overexposed and rendered the illumination source uncertain, and as a result, we make assumptions about how the dress was illuminated, which affects the colors we see" (Wallisch, 2017, p. 5).

This study unveiled the perplexing responses to the dress color, and also helped to expose how different people react to events and use their experiences to try and understand uncertainty. By generating discussion about the person, context, and environment, new information emerged that the researchers connected to internal body clocks and their effect on the way we see colors differently.

The point is that perspective matters. The perspectives of different people on your team can illuminate an ambiguous situation in a whole new way.

By becoming more attuned to how your thoughts, perceptions, and actions are affected—directly or indirectly—by other people, as well as by other people's perceptions, social norms, and experiences, you will begin to see how those elements may influence and affect even other people's personalities, character, and expectations. A pebble in a pond can create far-reaching ripple effects, and that's why you need to expand your view into all three spheres of insight (individual, organizational, and environmental) for decision-making when you are within ambiguous situations.

Key Takeaways

$B = f(P, E)$. In the field of psychology, this is the formula that some organizational psychologists may have tattooed somewhere on their bodies, as this theory is important and fundamental to their craft. It is the important foundation of field theory and is an important concept for understanding person, context, and the environment. Embracing this concept can provide executives, HR, and organizational development professionals with a much-needed approach to managing change within an organization. To enable yourself and others to thrive in ambiguous environments, you will need to surround yourself with the elements and people who help build that capacity.

Support organizational learning. Organizational learning is the process of creating, retaining, and transferring knowledge within, around, and across the organization with the purpose of gaining experiences and knowledge. To create a learning organization, you need employees who want to contribute and learn through their experiences. But, by now, you will have realized that only employees can motivate themselves to learn; they can't be forced. Your job is to create the supportive and challenging environment that enables them to learn, respond to issues, be mindful of nuances, and build the capacity to embrace the ambiguity mindset.

Embrace learning agility. Being able to learn through ambiguity requires agility, risk taking, and deep motivation to seek and uncover new knowledge, and it builds the social intelligence for yourself and others. You must be able to reflect on your experiences and subsequently apply that learning when faced with new situations.

Use mind maps. Mind maps represent networked information that enables you to conduct visual learning and helps promote better understanding. They make it easier for you to structure your thinking patterns, and they enable you to create new connections, generate new ideas, and see the strategy-decision pathway when you're faced with fluid and dynamic circumstances.

Build culture richness. There is a growing sense of urgency that everyone needs to increase their understanding of people from diverse cultural and ethnic backgrounds. Conflicting ideas, differences in working styles and backgrounds, and varied communication patterns will slow down your company, but understanding those differences will actually speed up effective decision-making. Finding ways to work together effectively will enable you to thrive during messy issues that require a variety of viewpoints.

Be illuminated by different perceptions and biases. Sometimes, the simple biology and chemistry of our brain create different perceptions and build up biased thinking patterns. A strong sense of curiosity and the motivation to determine why differences exist will enable both real and perceived barriers to dissolve. Simply stated, you are not a mind reader. Don't pretend to know what the other person is thinking. You have to ask them what they're thinking if you wish to arrive at a mutual understanding.

· · · · · ·

CHAPTER 5

HARNESS THE STRATEGIC POWER OF DIVERSE NETWORKS

H arnessing the strategic power of diverse networks is an essential part of developing an ambiguity mindset. This fifth thinking and behavior strategy casts a bright light on how our executives work within all three spheres of insight—individual, organizational, and environmental.

When I conducted the executive interviews and focus groups, I was honored to have such intelligent, acclaimed professionals allow me to learn about how they think and behave when immersed in confusion, power struggles, ill-defined policies, and deeply entrenched conflicting views. It would be logical to assume, prior to the interviews, that the executives would define their ambiguity coping mechanisms as simply having in-depth business acumen, or being highly skilled in strategic planning, or having merger and acquisition expertise. However, those business terms were never mentioned—not even once.

In fact, our executives' narratives used different phrases, including the following: understand the power of connections, build a community or relationships, seek information in the network, build connections, find parallels, use direct and indirect pathways, seek nonlinear relationships, create diversity on the team, know and understand how to communicate across various groups, seek subject matter experts, seek social exchanges, understand how different cultures bring different ideas, and find the value sharing.

Why would the executives use such soft concepts to deal with seemingly risky and precarious situations, with so much at stake? The reason may lie in the innate nature of ambiguity, assumptions of strategy, the concept of wicked problems, and how concepts such as stakeholder engagement, communities of practice, and knowledge sharing are key to harnessing the strategy power of diverse networks.

STRATEGIC ASSUMPTIONS

Horst Rittel and Melvin Webber, from the University of California, Berkeley, use the term *wicked problems* to define pervasive issues in societal and cultural contexts that are difficult or even impossible to solve. This would include global issues, such as climate change, political disputes, poverty, the repercussions of the pandemic, drug trafficking, and social injustice, to name a few (Rittel & Webber, 1973).

Researchers, governments, and Fortune 500 companies are keen to understand more about wicked problems, such as the contributing factors and potential (if any) for preventive strategies, to avoid costly and prolonged discourse. Russell Ackoff discusses wicked problems as not actual problems but "societal messes and unstructured reality" (Ackoff,

1974, p. 117). Considering the maze of challenges within wicked problems, such as changing agents, complex human factors, required cross-disciplinary expertise, and the lack of knowledge sharing that affects the agenda and outcomes, it is important to learn more about what a wicked problem is before launching into how to tackle it.

Rittel and Webber (1973) developed ten characteristics that separate wicked problems from normal problems:

- There is no definite formulation of a wicked problem. Because the problem is ill defined, it is difficult to determine its structure or the information required to solve it.

- Wicked problems have no stopping rules. Because wicked problems are ever evolving, it is impossible to know when they are solved.

- Solutions to wicked problems are not true or false but better or worse. Wicked problems are difficult to solve; rather, you can only seek to make incremental positive or negative changes to the messy issues.

- There is no immediate and no ultimate test of a solution to a wicked problem. This means that it is difficult to conduct a pilot program to test the validity of a solution, because the variables keep changing, and there is no defined road map or guide to solving the problem.

- Every solution to a wicked problem is a one-shot operation. Because there is no opportunity to learn by trial and error, every attempt counts significantly.

- Wicked problems do not have an enumerable (or an exhaustively describable) set of potential solutions; nor is there a well-described set of permissible operations that may be incorporated into the plan. Essentially, the variables are so interconnected to the socioeconomic systems that small changes may cause a new system change.

- Every wicked problem is essentially unique.

- Every wicked problem can be considered to be a symptom of another (wicked) problem.

- The causes of a wicked problem can be explained in numerous ways. The choice of explanation determines the nature of the problem's resolution.

- The planner has a right to be wrong. The strategist in charge of addressing the wicked problem is allowed to make a hypothesis and must not be penalized when it turns out to be wrong.

Wicked problems cannot be managed like an engineering project, and researchers now advocate moving away from business-as-usual problem-solving and reductionism tactics and moving toward optimization of the systems thinking approach. Wicked problems are dynamic, and each issue will have links to many other socioenvironmental issues. These problems should be seen as evolving problems within a system of systems; those trying to solve them should be prepared for difficulty in identifying the issue—and also the solution.

Jonathan Rosenhead, from the London School of Economics, has conducted extensive research on using problem-solving techniques to solve wicked problems. He was trying to provide decision-making with systemic help in identifying an agreed-on framework for a problem. Rosenhead (1996) presents the following criteria as being necessary for dealing with wicked problems:

- Accommodate multiple alternative perspectives rather than prescribing single solutions.

- Function through group interactions rather than back-office calculations.

- Be transparent when generating ownership of the problems.

- Facilitate a graphical representation for the systematic, group exploration of a solution space.

- Focus on relationships between discrete alternatives rather than continuous variables.

- Concentrate on possibility rather than probability.

These criteria coincide with the strategies cited in the interviews with executives: multiple alternative perspectives, group interactions, ownership, group exploration, and focus on relationships. If you are experiencing wicked problems, it would be prudent to avoid engineering stringent processes or using singular viewpoints, linear thinking, or top-down decisions. Otherwise, you may end up solving the wrong problem, a portion of the problem, or nothing at all.

STRATEGY AND LEARNING

The world is simply moving and changing too fast to rely on a linear planning process. You need to continually scan the environment for the winning dynamic methods that spark corporate growth. Willie Pietersen, author of *Strategic Learning*, states that to succeed in the competitive and changing VUCA world, executives need to create a fundamental shift to a strategy model that changes the concepts of discipline into adaptability and planning into discovering (Pietersen, 2010). Strategic learning is about "doing the right things and involves making intelligent choices and clarifying where and how the organization will complete and create value creation. Planning, on the other hand, is concerned with logistical and financial rigor and does not produce breakthrough thinking, but it is predictable as it generates forecasts, blueprints, and budgets" (Pietersen, 2010, p. 12).

Planning definitely has its place, but it's integrated as a subset of strategy. The learning pillar is required, because there is too much information, too many creative sources, and too many intellectual resources in the spheres of insight that need to be absorbed. Focusing only on planning and budgets is leaving too much intelligence on the cutting room floor. Interestingly, Pietersen talks about how strategy and leadership are really about winning the hearts and minds of your teams in support of what needs to be done. This is a difficult mental model shift for many companies to embrace, I know.

WHY NETWORKS MATTER

Many companies' communication patterns are fragmented and siloed. The premise of segmenting important corporate information into the *only for those who need to know* category is subjective, and although this may keep sensitive information compartmentalized, it does nothing for building an agile and collective learning ethos within the company. There may be other issues that arise from a lack of knowledge sharing. When information is sparse or hard to find, employees are not able to make sense of ambiguous information, and they can't tap into the social intelligence to find colleagues who may have faced the same issue.

Consider a company that noticed several problems within their organization: a gap in their informational processes, an inability to capture various consultants' deliverables for meaningful synergy, and frustration among departments because of a lack of cross-sharing of knowledge. On the behavioral side, there was a silo mentality, a lack of trust to share information, and a lack of effort to coordinate knowledge sharing.

In a practical sense, the business began to feel as if every new initiative was totally unique. In fact, there were multiple examples of routine errors occurring; for example, one department was spending significant amounts of time and money securing vendor A's product, and neither company knew that other members of each of their companies were already deep into negotiations. It is not just your own knowledge sharing that you need to pay attention to. You also need to pay attention to what's happening within your own network and among your stakeholders.

A study completed by Garold Stasser and William Titus indicated that groups often make suboptimal decisions, because they tend to discuss and incorporate shared information at the expense of information that is not shared or that is unknown by the entire team (Stasser & Titus, 1985). In other words, groups are not able to take advantage of the expertise of their team members if they don't seek to discover unknown knowledge. Ask yourself when you last learned something new through a business email. More than likely, your business is using email for tracking conversations, directives, and information. You do not use email for brainstorming or for creative design-thinking sessions; you must meet face-to-face to give everyone a thinking space for discovering unknown information. However, like most business day-to-day processes, you end up spending 90 percent of your day answering emails.

This indicates that knowledge-sharing motivations within networks are especially important. For example, the expectancy-value theory predicts that people's willingness to act is directly affected by their expectations about the potential effects of their action. This theory means that if I share knowledge and find value, others will find value and share knowledge—a learned behavior.

Knowledge sharing and effective decision-making are components of the book *Built to Change: How to Achieve Sustainable Organizational Effectiveness*. The authors write, "Spreading knowledge and power across many people allows everyone to move in a new direction to process and respond to information quickly without requiring a tremendous amount of top-down direction" (Lawler & Worley, 2006, p. 19). The authors further argue that the best B2C businesses are the ones that put as many employees as possible in direct contact with the external environment.

In other words, employees should have few—if any—degrees of separation from external customers and should know those networks. This knowledge-sharing strategy puts multiple programs and initiatives into each employee's reach to make a difference. What's interesting is that, although the executives in our interviews were focused on understanding the person, context, and environment in true Lewin style—$B = f(P, E)$—they were also creating a *group asset network* and found the community and teams to provide powerful insights.

Dr. Kameron Lewis Levin, a professional learning expert, conducted a research study to explore fifteen millennial educators who work in a high-poverty urban charter network. The research sought to identify the factors that influenced the teachers' decisions to stay in their jobs and progress as leaders within a high-turnover environment. This is important, as Richard Ingersoll, professor of education from the University of Pennsylvania, stated that with over three decades of data, approximately 33 percent of teachers in American public schools leave the field in the first three years, and 50 percent of them leave in the first five years (Lewis Levin, 2021).

Lewis Levin's study on millennial educators was analyzed through four lenses: motivation for staying, how the teachers learn, what they learn, and their reactions to the pandemic. The major findings were that a strong majority of participants indicated they were motivated to stay in a high-attrition environment because they liked their colleagues, while an equal number cited the positive school culture as a contributing factor to their retention. A slight majority of participants answered that the 2020 pandemic provided an opportunity to be innovative. A majority of participants indicated a desire to develop their capacity for learning and leadership, and a strong majority of participants described they learned largely in informal ways by dialoguing with others and through observation (Lewis Levin, 2021).

Lewis Levin advocates for creating a strong work culture to retain employees. By focusing on creating a community of highly motivated teachers, the knowledge and decision-making architecture assists in ambiguous and uncertain times. The executives I interviewed expressed a strong intention to build a team of ambiguity thinkers and doers to ensure the team had adaptable mental models and was aligned to the architecture of interpersonal knowledge and decision-making. Their ethos was to increase the collective strength and influence to create a learning strategy of ambiguity thinking and behaviors within the organization.

SEEK DIVERSE STAKEHOLDER INSIGHTS

Monitoring stakeholders and their evolving interests and power is an important element of harnessing the network. Consider the approach used by Dutch citizens in 2015. Rather than sitting back and waiting for their government to take a slow approach to climate change recommendations, Dutch citizens filed a civil lawsuit in The Hague, claiming that the Dutch government's stance on climate change was illegal, and ordered the government to cut greenhouse gas emissions by at least

25 percent within five years (to 2020). The Dutch citizens then created a suitable strategy with their stakeholders, including the Urgenda Foundation, the environment nonprofit that filed the lawsuit on behalf of the Dutch citizens. And the citizens won.

Although most—if not all—executives conduct stakeholder analysis during calm times, it is also a crucial tool during periods of crisis. The urgency of the problem puts a sense of panic in even seasoned executives; however, taking the time to conduct periodic analysis shows how the environment may have shifted before or after a panic event. Unless you are actually tapping into your stakeholders' sentiments and how they are reacting to similar panic events, you are guessing about your stakeholders' changing motives.

On a similar theme, Marwan, the conglomerate executive, spoke explicitly about the UAE context in terms of gaining information from the organizational and environmental spheres to help formulate the meaning of an experience. Marwan regularly works with consultants and said that they regularly drew on the office walls—massive whiteboards—to discuss various thinking styles and alternative ways to view a problem. Marwan also indicated a unique UAE cultural practice of visiting the *majalis*, which is an Arabic term for a gathering place where community members discuss events, socialize, and exchange ideas. He seeks to gain more insights into large- and small-scale shifts that may occur in the region or globally that might affect his own thinking style when faced with ambiguity. He said, "Getting information is important, and here in the UAE, visiting the *majalis* is how you get information. It might be rumor, but more than likely, it is a new idea. Eventually you confirm the information. I try to organize the information and ask more questions to lower the risk of uncertainty." Our transportation executive Luc learned the power of diverse stakeholders early in life. He attributed his ability to understand, to be able to hear, and to be able to speak to new people to his early days in boarding school. He was living with people from different parts of the world, and he had to quickly adapt and learn how to interact, socialize, and make friends. Now, being comfortable navigating megatrends is reshaping how countries interact with the dynamic transportation sector.

When faced with inconsistent data, a lack of information, or even an overload of conflicting information, uncertainty can begin to loom large and feel real. You can learn to absorb the anxiety of chaos by consciously making sense with other people. Together, you verify which information is the most effective to embrace for the next decision.

THE SOCIAL NETWORK EFFECT

I was involved in a dynamic network analysis assessment whereby my colleagues and I completed an array of questions regarding our preferences, values, and understanding of information. Social network analysis (SNA) is an evaluation approach that uses mathematics and visualization to represent the structure of relationships between people, organizations, goals, interests, and other entities within a larger system (Hoppe & Reinelt, 2010). The analysis results were used to identify our preferred processes and structures and to find a hidden pool of talent, subject matter experts, and rising stars. The network assessment draws on the thinking patterns within the system and on network dynamics to identify how people collaborate, share information, solve problems, and get work done. You have all seen the hierarchical organization charts that show how you are supposed to communicate for approvals, but they do nothing to clarify how to actually share information when hemmed in by power structures and segmented department communication methods.

Figure 8 shows how the organization functions and where it might face risks. It exposes knowledge gaps and who or how many people are the corporate connectors who help build the strongest communication links in your organization. In your own network, who usually has the most information? Where do you think they get the information? The connectors are the people who know and understand the dynamics of people, behaviors, and information and tap into the social sphere to see what has changed, what is new information, and how this new information creates value. More than likely, these corporate connectors have already found the value of reaching outside their individual spheres and make it part of their daily mantra to seek unknown information by talking to other people and joining diverse groups, teams, and clubs.

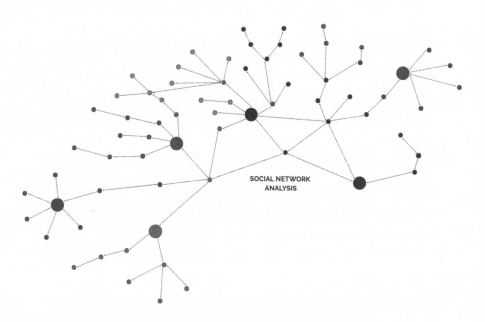

FIGURE 8. SOCIAL NETWORK ANALYSIS

In this context, the social network effect featured heavily in the executives' narratives. Hazel, the entrepreneur executive, talked about her early years and about knowing that knowledge transfer was important.

She stated, "I was living in Africa, and we had a housekeeper with eight children who was only allowed to send four of his children to school. I remember when I was five years old, I would come home from school and go to the bottom of the garden, and I would teach his kids what I had learned that day at school. So there was this early desire to share or transfer knowledge."

Additionally, the narratives also assigned value to stakeholder relationships and found early learning helped. Luc, the transportation executive, stated, "When I was in international school, those years taught me a lot about people. It was all relationship based. I do that now as well. If I have people coming from overseas to my home country, and if I'm there, invariably, I will always take them to my home. I would always have dinner for them. I would never think that it was a waste of effort, because it always comes back to assist you."

You should begin to find comfort in the unknown by finding mechanisms that allow you to interact with other networks—maybe not in the overt sense but in times of ambiguity. Try using the various ambiguity thinking and behavior strategies that are now at your disposal.

AMBIGUOUS SITUATED LEARNING

Situated learning is an approach developed by education theorists Jean Lave and Etienne Wenger in the early 1990s. They posited that people are more inclined to learn by actively participating with others in the learning experience. This includes situations such as site visits, learning activities in the classroom, internships, clubs, sports, and other settings in which people learn by making meaning from real activities (Lave & Wenger, 1991). Informal and incidental learning is required to help understand and reflect on the complexity and social context of all the interactions (Marsick et al., 2016). Essentially, situated learning explains how you can acquire experiences on how to be a good team member by playing on a soccer team or with another group or activity, by interacting with others in each situation.

You learn through relationships between people and through the authentic, informal, and often unintended contextual situations. There was an invisible space in the executive interviews in which they discussed creating the right environment to let the other members of a team learn through the executives' experiences but also in the challenging environment they all were immersed in. For example, Marcus, the shipping executive, stated, "As a business leader, you have to understand your environment and must have the right networks to do your business. Try to add value to the society around you—social economic value or maybe even political value. Then, I think you add value to those around you and develop a system."

Rachid, the oil and gas executive, added, "Building a future team, you take stock of resources you bring to the table and find a way to piece together the teams' learned experiences, that basket of offering that is impactful and sustainable."

This notion is supported by a research study conducted by Inger Beate Pettersen and Elin Kubberod. They explored situated ambiguity in students' entrepreneurial learning. The researchers wanted to address two questions: (1) How does situated ambiguity induced by a foreign culture contribute to contextual entrepreneurial learning in education? (2) Does ambiguity induced by cross-cultural experience stimulate critical reflection and learning outcomes and increase entrepreneurial self-efficacy? (Pettersen & Kubberod, 2017).

Norwegian School of Entrepreneurship students were introduced to internships in Singapore, Boston, Houston, San Francisco, and Cape Town. The findings revealed that the cultural learning settings enhanced the interns' understanding of ambiguity and uncertainty, and the students managed to adapt to different new methods to cope in the new environment. When immersed within ambiguity, learning through the different encounters and relationships within the spheres of insight help shape your responses (Pettersen & Kubberod, 2017).

While I interviewed the executives and learned about their experiences working in complex adaptive systems and large-scale start-up companies, they all provided a deep sense of being aware that they are constantly shifting and evolving from the interactions with others, both inside the organization and with the multicultural environment in the UAE. Our health care executives were tackling the complicated challenges of triage processes, interacting departments, a diverse workforce, nonalignment of information systems, and the community at large—patients with different backgrounds of health care experiences and standards. Amy stated, "In emergency nursing, it's a microcosm of the whole. It has its own little ecosystem, but it exists in the larger system at the hospital. You need to make sense of the overall system performance, using all the information you have to improve the situation. One of the practices I found most effective for leadership was *teaming*. You create microteams of different specialties to learn from each situation."

COMMUNITY OF PRACTICE

When tapping into the social intelligence of your networks, the concept of communities of practice is also a method of cultivating ambiguity insights. A *community of practice* is a group of self-organizing people creating binding relationships of mutual engagement. They build a relationship by practicing, learning, and innovating through talented, insightful, and diverse viewpoints. A community of practice is an extension of the situated learning theory; it is the collective learning gained *through social participation* and is the collaborative structure in which learning takes place (Lave & Wenger, 1991). The premise is to cultivate knowledge sharing in informal power structures to harvest rich contributions from people with multiple worldviews.

The community of practice and situated learning theories emphasize that learning and reflective practice are unintended and situated within authentic activities, their context, and the organization's culture. Lave and Wenger also stated that social interaction is a critical component of situated learning (Lave & Wenger, 1991). Employees who become involved in the community of practice within their organization learn from the interaction in an informal manner; learning is unintentional rather than deliberate. Workplace learning is inextricably linked with the work and the environment, and social contexts are important influences on learning.

When differing parties come together, their collective intellect spans a range of fields. Communities of practice have also been created with systems thinking methodologies in mind, created as thinking spaces where subject matter experts come together outside of their normal operational confines to brainstorm solutions. This refreshes them if their current thinking is stale or routine.

Global roundtables, new software apps such as Clubhouse, and other social platforms seek to bring thousands—if not millions—of energetic thinkers together from various industries and backgrounds to co-create for a brief period of time. Executives are realizing that more diverse networks are needed to solve complex issues and to create a shared sense of purpose.

The problem? It takes time and effort to hear all those differing voices and conflicting agendas. The goal of collecting data and learning that comes from different viewpoints is not to ensure everyone's input is added to strategy. Rather, the inputs are categorized to verify the emergent issues that need a mitigation strategy so that options are available when the surprises occur.

The interviewed executives were strong advocates of knowing that corporate value is increased when they are able to leverage the knowledge inside and across the organization to assist with effective decision-making. The ability to leverage knowledge is paramount when confronting ambiguous situations, because the know-what, know-why, know-how, and know-who spans across the organization.

ADVOCATING FOR WIN-WIN

Another aspect of harnessing the power of diverse networks is to learn how to build internal coalitions and department cross-collaboration. I was involved in a negotiation game facilitated by Deborah Kolb, former executive director of the Program on Negotiation at Harvard Law School, and Judith Williams, authors of *Everyday Negotiation: Navigating the Hidden Agendas in Bargaining*. The premise of the game (and the book) was to show how the participants involved in various negotiations can become more effective in their everyday negotiations by attending to the dual requirements of the shadow negotiation—advocacy for one-self but, more importantly, building connections with others (Kolb & Williams, 2003). Like other strategy, negotiation, or sales games, this one was about harnessing the power of diverse networks to seek knowledge and learn about the dynamics of the people you're working with. If you are stuck in your executive tower and speaking to only a few of your trusted sources, expand your network to include people who do not share the same perspectives. You don't need to like what you hear to be able to learn from it.

As soon as you sit down with more than two people, chances are that coalitions will form. Coalition building is a process of bringing together knowledgeable people who represent varying interests on an issue. The purpose of a coalition is to create focused dialogue, find common ground, and work together to advance mutually beneficial agendas. Building trust, seeking mutual benefits, and bridging multiparty agendas are intrinsic actions that can work in concert with knowledge sharing for effective decision-making.

To avoid corporate surprise barriers, learn to build coalitions and break down opposing ones. When a group of stakeholders seek to block a project, they may not be truly interested in blocking it. They may, instead, consciously or unconsciously be using tactics such as ambivalence, apathy, or disinterest. The goal is to provide incentives that change this behavior and potentially bring them into your coalition; they can then influence their direct reports and their own oppositional coalition to come around.

As the fifth strategy for developing an ambiguity mindset, harness the strategic power of diverse networks; access the power to understand uncertainty within ambiguous situations by reaching far outside your own framework. You will be able to find partial observations, glean insights from patterns, or relate similar clues to your previous experiences to build a strategic learning pathway through your messy situation.

Key Takeaways

Implement knowledge sharing. Knowledge sharing is not intuitive, and people seem to always undervalue the importance of mechanisms that enable the strategy to be permeated throughout the organization. Knowledge sharing is essential for making sense and for uncovering hidden value. This includes paying attention to knowledge-sharing mechanisms and organizational behaviors.

Embrace strategic learning. Strategic learning aims to generate learning to support future strategic initiatives, foster knowledge-sharing networks, and leverage formation technologies to improve organization performance. Because of the high levels of uncertainty and ambiguity and the fluid and dynamic changes that occur in all spheres of insight, you should embrace the dynamic cycle of four steps: learn, focus, align, and execute. And then repeat the process to be ready for unintended consequences.

Build a community of practice. A community of practice is a group of people who share a common concern and learn how to do things better as they interact regularly. This type of diverse group contains skills, expertise, and knowledge that build connections and informational nodes.

Harness the social network effect. The social network effect refers to the connections of your set of relationships, personal interactions, and connections. Once the network is expanded and strengthened, information flows. This enables unknown or hidden information to be shared. In complex adaptive systems, the social network includes the network itself, information circulation, friends and acquisitions, business networks, and difficult working relationships. You must analyze the links to verify where the key connectors are.

CHAPTER 6

· · · · ·

YOUR LEADERSHIP LEGACY

What is your ambiguity story? Are you challenged with solving a product launch issue, dealing with a strategic growth dilemma, or investigating troublesome manufacturing inefficiencies? Or has the pandemic provided a sliver of entrepreneurial hope for your business idea, although the path is fraught with too many unknowns? Alternatively, you may just want more clarity on how to decide on your next career move, build resilience for minor or major setbacks, or open a new branch office in a foreign country. Moving forward, when you are faced with a puzzling pattern of events, are stuck in a confusing situation, or feel trapped in your own routine thinking patterns, you now have more insights on how to develop your ambiguity mindset to create clarity for your next step.

On your ambiguity mindset journey, you have learned about the three decoding principles and the four components of an ambiguity mindset, and you have learned how to build the cognitive and behavioral capacity to adapt to new perspectives. You also know how to seek meaning from dynamic connections, interactions, experiences, and behaviors so as to determine the ideal decision pathway.

You have also learned more about how to view the world through the lenses of adult learning, organizational behaviors, and systems thinking. And through the three research questions, you have learned how dozens of top-level executives have worked through ambiguous situations while working in complex adaptive systems that point toward the five ambiguity thinking and behavior strategies:

- Create powerful insights through critical reflection.

- Cultivate adaptable mental models.

- Develop comfort in the unknown.

- Learn through person, context, and environment.

- Harness the strategic power of diverse networks.

So what now? I am primarily an academic-practitioner executive, which means that I continually seek to close the gap between theory and practical application, with a strong focus on how to operationalize theories into the workplace. Therefore, I expect there are at least three overarching barriers you might face when attempting to implement the five ambiguity thinking and behavior strategies. These three barriers include unmasking your ego and the illusion of control, determining how to disambiguate your stress, and changing your perceptions of time. Additionally, let's review a concept we have only briefly mentioned— leadership and your leadership legacy.

We close by revisiting the three research questions to collate many of the key insights you have learned. At the end of the book, Appendix A allows you to revisit the self-assessment questionnaire so you can gauge your comfort level and see if you've changed in how you'd cope with future ambiguous situations. Appendices B, C, D, and E include templates you and your HR and talent development teams can use to create stronger partnerships to implement organizational learning and to improve the mechanisms within your organization. By addressing these barriers, your leadership legacy, and a summary of all the knowledge you have gained, you are prepared to build resilience, wisdom, and mindfulness to resolve any future ambiguous situations.

UNMASKING THE EGO AND THE ILLUSION OF CONTROL

Even with all the overwhelming evidence showing that complex adaptive systems require adaptable mental models and that you must work within your spheres of insight to reach an informed decision pathway, your ego may still trip you up.

Although Sigmund Freud posited that the ego is the part of the personality that balances your internal desires with society's moral and social standards, in this case, I am referring to the concept of ego that refers to the conscious, decision-making part of your thinking process that you regard as *I*—essentially, the center of your universe: you.

You can identify your own ego state when you behave egoistically or egocentrically—when you are pursuing your own goals at the expense of others. As an executive, you may find that your ego is aligned to your professional identity, and understandably, this can make it hard to move away from the *I* perspective. Your leadership agenda may be under scrutiny, your confidence has been built in your ability to lead and make fast decisions, and your corporate and financial achievements may be high on your priority list. However, you have now learned that unilateral decisions and the sheer force of a command-and-control mandate cannot be leveraged when dealing with ambiguity. You have learned that, because of your cognitive bias and the illusion of control, you will have the tendency to overestimate your control of events and people. You have also learned to release your need for perfection during conditions of ambiguity.

You have absorbed the fact that hierarchy control is not real control, and you know how to be a systems thinker to understand the dynamic changes that occur throughout the organization. You understand that you have blind spots and assumptions and may have stubborn viewpoints, but you have gained insights into how you can uncover your biases to become more flexible in your mental models by adopting tools such as the ladder of inference, the Johari window, lessons-learned activities, and reflection both in and on action techniques.

You have also learned that you can quickly scan your environment for feedback, gain context, and learn from previous experiences to make sense of the uncertainty. You have gained insights that expanding your point of view and building a wide-angle lens, and reflecting critically on those insights, will broaden your proposed solution.

If you have been writing in your journal while reading this book, you will have found patterns in your negative and positive thinking and behavior that will provide self-awareness insights. You now have many different tools and resources at your disposal to ensure that you are reflecting critically to enable you and your team to succeed, despite your different viewpoints and experiences.

DISAMBIGUATE YOUR STRESS

Despite the plethora of mindful and mental health research at your fingertips, you will still succumb to stress when faced with ambiguous situations unless you understand your stress triggers. This means when you are stuck in a stressful situation, such as when your board members or your boss's boss is relying on you to get the project done by tomorrow, you must incorporate the ambiguity thinking and behavior coping mechanisms. You have learned more about emotional intelligence and your own and others' emotions during times of stress and when dealing with emotional information. You have developed emotional intelligence key points to descope the emotions from the situation, such as how to be an *object* rather than a *subject* in difficult situations. This enables a better assessment of the situation.

You have learned that, when you are stressed, you may have slower reaction times when making decisions and that any acute stress will increase your cognitive load—meaning that the burden of your thinking turns cloudy. You now understand that linear, fast-paced decision-making will create recurring or systemic errors and that, by turning toward curiosity, you will ask the right questions from your network and community. You know, too, that you can examine your previous ambiguity experiences to help you develop workable solutions.

You have learned that being curious reduces stress behaviors, such as fight or flight. You have also learned that ambiguity slips away when you tap into the social, cultural, and network richness of information and when you illuminate diverse viewpoints to provide more clarity to your uncertain situation.

PERCEPTIONS OF TIME

Complex adaptive systems and the dynamic work environment place enormous pressure on you to complete your job deliverables. Quite frankly, it is probably easier for you to do the majority of your job yourself—without collaborating with people and trying to understand their thinking or behavior patterns. The rush to deliver and to achieve your targets has trained you to plan and detail all your time in advance. However, the nuances of ambiguity and uncertainty require you to pay attention and devote time and effort to take deliberate pauses, to pay attention to the chaos of the ten thousand butterflies to see the patterns, and to step outside of your technical role to become better at understanding people and behaviors.

But you have also learned the value of mind mapping and how to carve out some time and space to see the invisible and important collaborative links that affect your business outcomes. You have learned how social intelligence can provide you with rich insights that may help create more well-rounded solutions, despite the time it takes to meet and learn within diverse groups of people. You have also learned more about executive coaching and the value of taking at least one hour per month to gain deeper and long-lasting clarity.

YOUR LEADERSHIP LEGACY

There is no specific section titled *leadership* in this book, but it could be argued that an ambiguity mindset and the thinking and behavior strategies could be classified as leadership competencies. I encourage you to link the concept of leadership to an ambiguity mindset to achieve your highest level of professional capacity.

Learning more about leadership is a deep, comprehensive, and sometimes confusing endeavor, because there are multiple definitions of what leadership is. However, it is widely agreed that Peter Northouse, author of *Leadership: Theory and Practice*, defines it best. Northouse states that leadership is "a process whereby an individual influences a group of individuals to achieve a common goal" (Northouse, 2015, p. 3). Your thinking and behavior patterns when faced with ambiguity must bring your teams along to help achieve the goals. Leadership is not a skill that is practiced in a vacuum.

Nor is building your leadership skills a one-and-done exercise. Rather, you can visualize it as drops of leadership insights filling a deep bucket. You continually need to keep filling the bucket with new or refined skills. You have learned the power of executive coaching to help you uncover hidden biases, to become empowered, to help improve lives, and to enrich relationships and business performance. Executive coaches help you set goals for transformational change and explore your journey.

There is a plethora of leadership books, articles, and blogs readily available that provide literal reams of information on what good leadership looks like. For example, you can read any number of leadership books, such as *The 7 Habits of Highly Effective People* by Stephen Covey, *Good to Great* by Jim Collins, *Thinking, Fast and Slow* by Daniel Kahneman, *Think Again* by Adam Grant, *The Five Dysfunctions of a Team* by Patrick Lencioni, *Multipliers* by Liz Wiseman and Greg McKeown, and so many other amazing works by authors who have researched leadership. You can also attend courses on executive leadership and strategy, which are often accessible online, including those offered by Columbia University and INSEAD. You can even seek out other world-class executive leadership and strategy programs such as the Center of Creative Leadership (CCL).

However, if you are an executive who has not taken a leadership course in a while, has not participated in a 360° review, or has not taken the opportunity to find your blind spots with an executive coach, you may not be living up to your executive and leadership potential for yourself or for others.

But I get it. It is difficult to focus on collaboration, engagement, building trust, and motivating others when you have overwhelming pressure from the board and your demanding corporate partnerships. However, the world is already filled with examples of hard-nosed executives with impressive financial achievements who have felt unfulfilled at the end of their career, as they didn't focus on the people or create any meaningful people experiences. I am talking about your leadership legacy, not corporate financial achievements. Layoffs and budget cuts are dead easy. Anyone can do that to meet short-term targets.

Leaving a leadership legacy is different. It is the story of your lifetime of achievements that includes your impact on the lives of the people around you when immersed in confusion. Your leadership legacy is how people talk about you when you leave the room and how you deal with the paradoxes of conflicting messages. Your leadership legacy is how you use inspiring guiding principles within your discussions and actions. It is how you help guide the company and your teams through uncertainty and ambiguous disruptions.

I hope you embrace the methodologies of the research and the elites who operate in conditions of ambiguity, and model these five thinking and behavior strategies. To summarize, let's revisit the three research questions to collate the tools and resources at your disposal and ensure the five ambiguity thinking and behavior strategies fill your tool kit.

THE SUM OF ALL MOVING PARTS

There were three research questions that helped us identify the components of an ambiguity mindset.

The first research question—*What are the beliefs, behaviors, and principles of business executives who work in conditions of ambiguity?*—led to the first two ambiguity mindset thinking and behavior strategies: Create powerful insights through critical reflection, and cultivate adaptable mental models. The executives' beliefs and behaviors point to the act of critical reflection, which enables the executives to build mental model flexibility. The narratives supported the link between thinking, learning, and action from different experiences and influences, rather than solely from their own point of view.

First, the data pointed to a flexible cognitive process that was in play, whereby the executives adapted their mental models to the context and were continually constructing knowledge through each experience or situation to provide better thinking strategies. The executives' adapting mental models are based on various social, cultural, relational, and reflective attributes. These sociocognitive influences help explain why the executives were able to successfully navigate within complex adaptive systems.

Second, certain behaviors are an important part of this cognitive intellectual activity. The executives displayed a high degree of will to learn and adapt to uncertain situations. The three main behavior traits derived from the narratives and theories were the following:

- They sought meaning from the experiences and used sensemaking attributes.

- They directed the dynamic and critical communication mechanisms within the system to capture information and knowledge.

- They built connections among the stakeholders within the systems.

This last point suggests that the executives were able to turn their thinking strategies into action by using dialogue and building their network to promote an action that is part of an ambiguity mindset.

Finally, as proposed by Kurt Lewin (1936), if behavior is a function of the interaction of the person and the environment, the executives were at the forefront of having to adapt their behavior on a continual basis because of the complex adaptive system elements that contain changing behaviors and environments. The proposal is relevant to how the executives navigated in complex adaptive systems and built their adaptive mental models. Therefore, a large component of an ambiguity mindset includes the cognitive learning and knowledge architecture of critical reflective practice, adaptable mental models, and action-oriented behaviors.

The second research question—*What experiences and events provide the scaffolding in the development of an ambiguity mindset?*—pointed to the ambiguity thinking and behavior strategy of developing comfort in the unknown. These are the informal learning experiences that occur in ambiguous situations that offer a strategic learning pathway. There were three broad types of experiences that built the executives' ambiguity mindset:

- Becoming involved in ambiguous situations
- Being exposed to alternative ways of thinking
- Being involved with people who challenge assumptions

If you lean into these types of events and situations, the informal learning experiences, the situations that scare you, or the unique problems that have no definitive decision pathway, you will build your capacity for an ambiguity mindset. This means volunteering for the tough projects at work, building forward-thinking internship programs for your company to build awareness among younger employees, and providing your employees with ambiguous stretch projects that test their mettle. This is the partnership that executives and the HR and talent teams must co-create to build corporation-wide mental strength.

The third research question—*What relationships, systems, and elements in the environment enable executives to develop the capacity to think through ambiguity?*—provided insight into the remaining two ambiguity thinking and behavior strategies: learning through people, context, and the environment and harnessing the strategic power of diverse networks.

These elements helped build organizational capacity and described how the social, cultural, and community practices were strong influences that enabled the executives to navigate ambiguity, social context, and complexity.

Also, learning from how people interact, promote dialogue, or share information by adopting a strategic learning component was instrumental in the executives' abilities to influence their various behaviors and thinking patterns. The three spheres of insight—individual, organizational, and environmental—encompass the social and cultural environments of how executives can build their cognitive intellectual capacity by understanding people and the environment.

Through the decoding principles and the five ambiguity thinking and behavior strategies, you have also learned how forward-thinking corporations, adult educators, and leadership practitioners are building their understanding for these concepts. They foster the following assumptions to understand and deal with the many uncertainties, decision pathways, and unintended consequences that may occur on your journey:

- Mental models adapt to ambiguity and uncertain situations.

- Certain action-oriented behaviors are part of this intellectual capacity.

- Informal learning experiences in ambiguous and uncertain situations provide an ambiguity learning pathway.

- Learning through social, cultural, and operational systems and the spheres of insight is an underused strategy.

As an executive, you now have all the research to show that you are in a position to capture additional growth and cognitive capacity, and to learn how to learn from your experiences. You can now do something amazing with that knowledge. Now you can act on your new knowledge with the key behaviors to build an ambiguity mindset for yourself and others in your organization.

IN SUMMARY

You have now learned the five behavior and thinking strategies that enable you to develop an ambiguity mindset. You understand ambiguity and uncertainty to a higher degree. By incorporating these theories, tools, and resources, you will build incremental adjustments to your thinking and behavior patterns. With the purpose of learning from your experiences, seeking challenges, and adopting a wide range of mental models and viewpoints, your enhanced ambiguity mindset will be a dynamic tool for excelling in complex adaptive systems.

I hope you enjoyed the executives' narratives of their ambiguity thinking and behavior patterns and that you were able to relate to their experiences. I leave you now with the ambiguity mindset overview and other templates in the appendices that you can incorporate into your personal portfolio or as a corporate blueprint to create your own learning organization.

ACKNOWLEDGMENTS

This book is dedicated to my husband, John Sutherland, who provided the unending support in my continuous learning and writing journey, who was always there to listen to my thoughts, who provided encouragement when my mental roadblocks took hold, and who was the foundation that enabled me to reach so many milestone achievements. I also share this dedication with my adult children, Bailey and Jake Sutherland, who provided the positive enthusiasm and interest in my book and never wavered from their chant: "You can do this!" I am full of gratitude for their love and support.

Additionally, a special thank-you goes to my mother, Jean Tkatch, who never stopped me from exploring the world as a young adult, which started me on the worldview learning path, and to my sister, Shelley Tkatch, who was always willing to share a knowing nod about the paradoxes of life.

I extend a massive thank-you to the interviewed executives, who were the richest source of content for my research, for being so generous with their time and insights. I am forever enlightened by their calm and intelligent voices as I wrote this book. They are truly amazing, humble leaders. My gratitude extends to all the executives who participated in the pilot studies and focus groups. I also thank my past colleagues for providing me with collaboration and discussion that offered so many rich insights.

In addition, I thank the XMA and AEGIS faculty at Teachers College, Columbia University, who were instrumental in enabling me to expand my thinking capabilities and provided intellectual support and confidence in my work. And I am grateful to my truly amazing cohorts, who enriched the learning journey in so many ways.

Of course, this book would not be possible without Greenleaf Book Group's stellar editorial, marketing, sales, and artistic teams, who were incredibly professional and knowledgeable and made me feel that my book was special. I extend a warm thank-you to Daniel Sandoval for believing in this business psychology book topic and the amazing editorial and design team: Nathan True, Pam Nordberg, and Teresa Muniz.

. . . . .

DEALING WITH AMBIGUITY: A SELF-ASSESSMENT QUESTIONNAIRE

P lace an X in the number space that relates best to your current comfort level on each question, with the following scale: 1, very uncomfortable; 2, somewhat uncomfortable; 3, comfortable; 4, somewhat comfortable; 5, very comfortable. The questions relate to the three decoding principles.

RATE YOUR COMFORT LEVEL FOR THE FOLLOWING AREAS:	1	2	3	4	5
To acknowledge that "not knowing" is okay during unexpected situations					
To embrace inexactness, paradoxes, or uncertain situations					
To take the time needed to understand the potential consequences of faulty perspective taking					
To compare own perspective with diverse or alternative views to verify differences					
To explore the different behaviors in the workplace or the systems you are in					
To resist making quick decisions and delay providing a response					
To adapt project direction with unstructured or unclear schedules or targets					
To be curious in knowledge gap situations					
To seek to work or live in uncertain, chaotic, or unstructured environments					
To find different social networks to find conflicting or paradoxical information					
To adopt new attitudes or behaviors from different cultural beliefs					
To be prepared to learn new things when faced with unfamiliar situations					

. . . . .

CRITICAL REFLECTION JOURNAL PROMPTS

Individual sphere reflection

- What were my emotional triggers when I was immersed in the confusion?

- What is my intention to learn today to help me understand the situation?

- What strong behaviors did I exhibit and in what context during the uncertain situation?

- What assumptions did I hold regarding the difficult situation?

- How did I positively or negatively influence any outcomes?

Organizational sphere reflection

- How did I interact with the team when we were in the messy situation?

- What perspectives seem to be missing or not heard?

- What emotions were on display from others? And what were the triggers?

Environmental sphere reflection

- What did I learn today about power and authority?

- What did I learn today about others when immersed in ambiguous and uncertain environments?

- What is the power structure at play here?

. . . . .

MY DINNER PARTY

I magine that you are going to throw a dinner party and will invite eight of your closest family and friends. This dinner party is going to be a bit different, though. Instead of having a dinner of different food dishes, you are going to ask your family and friends to each bring a piece of personal or professional advice they feel would benefit you. Place your responses in the right column:

List all the people you would invite to the dinner party.	
If each of the guests were to bring you a piece of advice that they think you would benefit from, list the advice you think they would bring.	
Select the pieces of advice that resonate with you and that you feel are beneficial to pursue.	
List the obvious barriers to achieving the newfound goals.	
List the ways to overcome the barriers to achieving the newfound goals.	
Write two positive phrases that create your new frame of reference.	
Now list your goals and the steps needed to achieve them.	

· · · · ·

COMPREHENSIVE REVIEW CHART

OPEN SYSTEMS, OPEN MINDS		
Decoding principle 1: View the world through a wide-angle lens; learn your own blind spots, assumptions, and biases.	Decoding principle 2: Learn your behavior and thinking architecture; see the context, systems, and situation around you.	Decoding principle 3: Learn from unfamiliar experiences; learn from environment, community, and networks.
SPHERES OF INSIGHT		
Individual	Organizational	Environment

FOUNDATIONAL CONCEPTS			
Mental models • Beliefs • Sense making • Reflection • Assumptions • Social constructs • Worldviews	Systems thinking • Whole rather than parts • Feedback loops • Open systems • Dynamic behavior • Systems structure as the cause of behavior	Complex adaptive systems • Changing agents • Rapid and dynamic shifts • Self-organizing • Nonlinear relationships • Interconnections/ interrelationships	Learning from experience • Social constructivist perspective • Reflection in/ on experience • Making meaning from experiences • Social and situational context

FIVE AMBIGUITY THINKING AND BEHAVIOR STRATEGIES		
#1: Create powerful insights through critical reflection.	Thinking strategies • Critical reflection • Creating meaning from experiences • Self-awareness • Subject-object perspective	Behavior strategies • Challenging assumptions • Reflection in/on action • 360° reviews • Reflective journaling
#2: Cultivate adaptable mental models.	Thinking strategies • Double-loop learning • Challenging self-assumptions (My Dinner Party) • Social constructivism	Behavior strategies • Seeking meaning and sensemaking attributes • Promoting critical dialogue • Fostering crucial connections • Ladder of inference
#3: Develop comfort in the unknown.	Thinking strategies • Emotional intelligence • Demystifying the fear • Exploring the knowing gap	Behavior strategies • Seeking ambiguous situations • Exposure to alternate ways of thinking • Challenging assumptions • Simulations • Strategic queries
#4: Learn through person, context, and environment.	Thinking strategies • $B = f(P, E)$ • Social intelligence • Learning agility • Motivational theories	Behavior strategies • Mind mapping • Organizational learning • Seeking cultural understanding • Illuminating insights from differences
#5: Harness the strategic power from diverse networks.	Thinking strategies • Awareness of wicked problems • Strategic assumptions • Knowledge sharing	Behavior strategies • Strategic learning • Community of practice • Building social network

• • • • •

AMBIGUITY
MINDSET MODEL

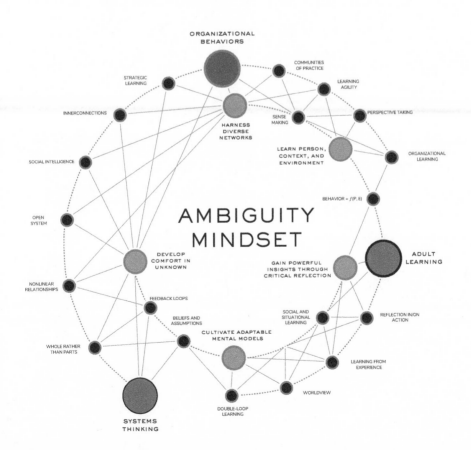

REFERENCES

Ackoff, R. L. (1974). *Redesigning the future: A systems approach to societal problems.* New York: Wiley.

Ackoff, R. L. (2015). Systems thinking speech by Dr. Russell Ackoff. Retrieved from https://www.youtube.com/watch?v=EbLh7rZ3rhU

Argyris, C. (1980). *Inner contradictions of rigorous research.* New York: Academic Press.

Argyris, C. (1982). *Reasoning, learning and action.* San Francisco, CA: Jossey Bass.

Argyris, C., & Schön, D. (1974). *Theory in practice: Increasing professional effectiveness.* San Francisco, CA: Jossey-Bass.

Big Think. (2012, April 23). Carol Gilligan on "In a different voice." https://www.youtube.com/watch?v=mG3_ZP6Drn0

Booth, P. K. (2019). *Behavior analysis: Catalyst for perspective transformation and perceptions of interpersonal effectiveness* (Doctoral dissertation, Teachers College, Columbia University, New York). https://academiccommons.columbia.edu/doi/10.7916/d8-c98a-c578

Boxer, R., Perren, L., & Berry, A. (2013). SME top management team and non-executive director cohesion: Precarious equilibrium through information asymmetry. *Journal of Small Business and Enterprise Development, 20*(1), 55–70. doi:10.1108/14626001311298411

Bronfenbrenner, U. (1994). Ecological models of human development. In T. Husen & T. N. Postlethwaite (Eds.), *International encyclopedia of education* (Vol. 3, 2nd ed., pp. 3–44). Oxford, UK: Elsevier.

Brooks, L., Dawkins, M., & Sutherland, D. (2017). *Exploring reflective journaling perspectives of driven women* (Unpublished manuscript, Teachers College, Columbia University, New York).

Budner, S. N. Y. (1962). Intolerance of ambiguity as a personality variable. *Personality, 30*(1), 29–50. doi:10.1111/j.1467-6494.1962.tb02303.x

Burke, W. W. (2017). Learning agility and how motivation drives change. *Talks at Columbia.* Retrieved from https://www.youtube.com/watch?v=ORQz5FadIio

Burke, W. W., Roloff, K. S., & Mitchinson, A. (2016). *Learning agility: A new model and measure* (White paper, Teachers College, Columbia University, New York).

Chrisomalis, C. V. (2021). *Mindset and feedback receptivity in a team facilitation setting: exploring factors perceived by adult educators that influence their learning in role* (Doctoral dissertation, Teacher's College, Columbia University, New York). https://academiccommons.columbia.edu/doi/10.7916/d8-z1jq-7p72

Dewey, J. (1933). *How we think.* Boston: D.C. Heath and Co.

Dewey, J. (1938). *Experience and education.* New York, NY: Collier.

Drath, W. (2001). *The deep blue sea: Rethinking the source of leadership.* San Francisco, CA: Jossey-Bass & Center for Creative Leadership.

Edmondson, A. C., & Harvey, J. F. (2017). *Extreme teaming: Lessons in complex, cross-sector leadership.* Bingley, UK: Emerald Publishing.

Eraut, M. (2000). Non-formal learning and tacit knowledge in professional work. *British Journal of Educational Psychology, 70,* 113–136.

Eurich, T. (2018, January). What self-awareness really is (and how to cultivate it). *Harvard Business Review.* https://hbr.org/2018/01/what-self-awareness-really -is-and-how-to-cultivate-it

Forrester, L. W. (1971). Counterintuitive behavior of social systems. *Technology Review, 73*(3), 52–68.

Frenkel-Brunswik, E. (1949). Intolerance of ambiguity as an emotional and perceptual personality variable. *Journal of Personality, 18*(1), 108–143. https://doi.org/10.1111 /j.1467-6494.1949.tb01236.x

Gawande, A. (2011, September 26). Personal best. *The New Yorker.* https://www .newyorker.com/magazine/2011/10/03/personal-best

Gironda, L. A. (2019). *Cross-Cultural practices of adult educators in blended global education* (Doctoral dissertation, Teacher's College, Columbia University, New York). https://academiccommons.columbia.edu/doi/10.7916/d8-xshj-1347

Green, D. W. (1996). Models, arguments, and decisions. In J. Oakhill & A. Garnham (Eds.), *Mental models in cognitive science: Essays in honor of Phil Johnson-Laird* (pp. 119–138). New York, NY: Psychology Press.

Heck, P. R., Simons, D. J., & Chabris, C. F. (2018). 65% of Americans believe they are above average in intelligence: Results of two nationally representative surveys. *PLoS ONE, 13*(7). http://doi.org/10.1371/journal.pone.0200103

Holland, J. H. (2005). Studying complex adaptive systems. *Journal of Systems Science and Complexity, 19*(1), 1–8. https://doi.org/10.1007/s11424-006-0001-z

Hoppe, B. & Reinelt, C. (2010). Social network analysis and the evaluation of leadership network. *The Leadership Quarterly, 21*, 600–619.

Kegan, R. (1994). *In over our heads*. Boston, MA: Harvard University Press.

Kelman, H. (1958). Compliance, identification, and internalization: Three processes of attitude change. *Journal of Conflict Resolution, 2*(1), 51–60.

Kets de Vries, M. (2018, October 1). The fine line between stubbornness and stupidity. *Knowledge*. https://knowledge.insead.edu/blog/insead-blog/the-fine-line -between-stubbornness-and-stupidity-10181

Knowles, M. (1970). *The modern practice of adult education: From pedagogy to andragogy*. New York, NY: Association Press.

Kolb, D. A. (1984). *Experiential learning: Experience as the source of learning and development*. Englewood Cliffs, NJ: Prentice-Hall.

Kolb, D. M., & Williams, J. (2003). *Everyday negotiation: Navigating the hidden agendas in bargaining*. San Francisco, CA: Jossey-Bass.

Krumboltz, J. D., & Levin, A. S. (2004). *Luck is no accident* (3rd ed.). San Luis Obispo, CA: Impact.

Kubberod, E., & Pettersen, I. B. (2017). Exploring situated ambiguity in students' entrepreneurial learning. *Education + Training, 59*(3), 265–279.

Lave, J., & Wenger, E. (1991). *Situated learning: Legitimate peripheral participation*. New York, NY: Cambridge University Press.

Lawler, E. E., & Worley, C. G. (2006). *Built to change: How to achieve sustained organizational effectiveness*. San Francisco, CA: Jossey-Bass.

Lewin, K. (1936). *Principles of topological psychology*. New York, NY: McGraw-Hill.

Lewis Levin, K. (2021). *Holding onto millennial teachers: Learning from aspiring leader's experiences* (Doctoral dissertation, Teacher's College, Columbia University, New York). https://academiccommons.columbia.edu/doi/10.7916/d8-dfvy-nm54

Lichtenstein, B. B., Uhl-Bein, M., Marion, R., Seers, A., Orton, J. D., & Schreiber, C. (2006). Complexity leadership theory: An interactive perspective on leading in complex adaptive systems. *Emergence: Complexity and Organization, 8*(4), 2–12. https://digitalcommons.unl.edu/cgi/viewcontent.cgi?referer=https://www.google .com/&httpsredir=1&article=1007&context=managementfacpub

Loftus, G. R. (1985). Evaluating forgetting curves. *Journal of Experimental Psychology: Learning, Memory and Cognition, 11*(2), 397–406.

Louis, M. R. (1980). Surprise and sense making: What newcomers experience in entering unfamiliar organizational settings. *Administrative Science Quarterly, 25*, 226–251.

Luft, J., & Ingham, H. (1955). The Johari window: A graphic model of interpersonal awareness. In *Proceedings of the Western Training Laboratory in Group Development*. Los Angeles: University of California, Los Angeles.

Marsick, V. J., & Watkins, K. E. (1990). *Informal and incidental learning in the workplace*. London, UK: Routledge.

Marsick, V. J., & Watkins, K. E. (2001). Informal and incidental learning. *New Directions for Adult and Continuing Education, 89*, 25–34.

Marsick, V. J., Watkins, K. E., Scully-Russ, E., & Nicolaides, A. (2016). Rethinking informal and incidental learning in terms of complexity and social context. *Journal of Adult Learning, Knowledge and Innovation, 1*(1), 27–34.

Merton, R. K. (1936). The unanticipated consequences of purposive social action. *American Sociological Review, 1*(6), 894–904.

Mezirow, J. (1991). How critical reflection triggers transformative learning. In J. Mezirow & Associates (Eds.), *Fostering Critical Reflection in Adulthood* (pp. 1–20). San Francisco, CA: Jossey-Bass.

Mintzberg, H. (1994). *The rise and fall of strategic planning: Reconceiving roles for planning, plans and planners*. New York, NY: The Free Press.

Niederer, I., Kriemier, S., Zahner, L., Burgl, F., Ebenegger, V., Hartman, T., Meye, U., Schindler, C., Nydegger, A., Marques-Vidal, P., & Puder, J. (2009). Influence of a lifestyle intervention in preschool children on physiological and psychological parameters (Ballabeina): Study design of a cluster randomized controlled trial. *BMC Public Health, 9*(1), 94. doi:10.1186/1471-2458-9-94

Northouse, P. G. (2015). *Leadership: Theory and practice*. Thousand Oaks, CA: Sage.

O'Dell, C., & Grayson, C. J. (1998). *If only we knew what we know: The transfer of internal knowledge and best practice*. New York, NY: The Free Press.

Owen, R. (2019). *Learning that meets life: The lived experience of teaching with secular spiritual pedagogy* (Doctoral dissertation, Teacher's College, Columbia University, New York). https://academiccommons.columbia.edu/doi/10.7916/d8-0421-jx97

Pasmore, Bill (2020). *Advanced consulting: Earning trust at the highest level*. Oakland, CA: Berrett-Koehler Publishers.

Pettersen, I. B., & Kubberod, E. (2017). Exploring situated ambiguity in students' entrepreneurial learning. *Education and Training, 59*(3). doi:10.1108/ET-04-2016-0076

Phillips, K. W. (2014). How diversity makes us smarter. *Scientific American, 311*(4). https://cdn.sfballet.org/2019/03/01221834/TEP-How-Diversity-Makes-Us-Smarter-Scientific-American.pdf

Piaget, J. (1966). *The psychology of intelligence* (M. Pierce & D. Berlyne, Trans.). New York, NY: Littlefield, Adams.

Pietersen, W. (2010). *Strategic learning: How to be smarter than your competition and turn key insights into competitive advantage.* Hoboken, NJ: Wiley.

Rashid, F., Edmondson, A. C., & Leonard H. B. (2013, July–August). Leadership lessons from the Chilean mine rescue. *Harvard Business Review.* https://hbr.org/2013/07/leadership-lessons-from-the-chilean-mine-rescue

Rehman, A. A. (2020). *How private equity professionals learn from experience: A qualitative study of 15 professionals.* (Doctoral dissertation, Teacher's College, Columbia University, New York). https://academiccommons.columbia.edu/doi/10.7916/d8-5gk9-dy10

Richmond, B. (1994). Systems thinking/systems dynamics: Let's just get on with it. *Systems Dynamics Review, 10,* 2–3.

Rittel, H. W., & Webber, M. M. (1973). Dilemmas in a general theory of planning. *Policy Sciences, 4,* 155–169.

Rock, D. (2009). Managing with the brain in mind. *Strategy + Business, 56.* https://www.strategy-business.com/article/09306

Rosenhead, J. (1996). What's the problem? An introduction to problem structuring methods. *Interfaces, 26*(6), 117–131.

Schön, D. A. (1983). *The reflective practitioner.* New York, NY: Basic Books.

Senge, P. (1990). *The fifth discipline.* New York, NY: Doubleday.

Starbuck, W. H., & Milliken, F. J. (1988). Executives' perceptual filters: What they notice and how they make sense. In D. C. Hambrick (Ed.), *The executive effect: Concepts and methods for studying top managers* (pp. 35–65). Greenwich, CT: JAL.

Stasser, G., & Titus, W. (1985). Pooling of unshared information in group decision making: Biased information sampling during discussion. *Journal of Personality and Social Psychology, 48*(6), 1467–1478.

Sweeney, L. B., & Sterman, J. D. (2000). Bathtub dynamics: Initial results of a systems thinking inventory. *System Dynamics Review, 16*(4), 249–286.

Systems Thinker. (2009). The ladder of inference. *Systems Thinker, 10*(8). https://thesystemsthinker.com/the-ladder-of-inference/

Taylor, K., & Marienau, C. (2016). *Facilitating learning with the adult brain in mind: A conceptual and practice guide.* San Francisco, CA: Jossey-Bass/Wiley.

Tropical Agriculture Platform. (2016). *Common framework on capacity development for agricultural innovation systems: Conceptual background.* Wallingford, UK: CAB International.

Vogt, E. (1995). Learning out of context. In S. Chawla & J. Renesch (Eds.), *Learning organizations: Developing cultures for tomorrow's workplace* (pp. 292–303). Portland, OR: Productivity Press.

Vygotsky, L. S. (1978). *Mind in society.* Cambridge, MA: Harvard University Press.

Wallisch, P. (2017). Illumination assumptions account for individual differences in the perceptual interpretation of a profoundly ambiguous stimulus in the color domain: The dress. *Journal of Vision, 17*(4), 5.

Weick, K. E. (1995). *Sensemaking in organizations.* Thousand Oaks, CA: Sage.

Wiseman, E., & McKeown, G. (2010). *Multipliers: How the best leaders make everyone smarter.* New York, NY: HarperCollins Publishers.

Wolfsfeld, L., & Haj-Yahia, M. M. (2010). Learning and supervisory styles in the training of social workers. *The Clinical Supervisor, 29*(1), 68–94. doi:10.1080/07325221003742066

Wong, J. C. (2019, April 12). Disgruntled drivers and "cultural challenges": Uber admits to its biggest risk factors. *The Guardian.* https://www.theguardian.com /technology/2019/apr/11/uber-ipo-risk-factors

World Economic Forum (2019). Insight report: The global competitiveness report, 2019. http://www3.weforum.org/docs/WEF_TheGlobalCompetitiveness Report2019.pdf

Yorks, L., & Nicolaides, A. (2013). Toward an integral approach for evolving mindsets for generative learning and timely action in the midst of ambiguity. *Teachers College Record, 115*(8), 1–26.

INDEX

Italic page numbers indicate pages with figures or tables.

A

abstract conceptualization (AC), 28, *28*
Ackoff, Russell, 9, 10, 124
active experimentation (AE), 28, *28*
Adam (real estate executive), 58–62, 83–84, 93–94
adaptable mental models, 49–74, 144, 151–153, 164. *See also* mental models
  challenging assumptions, 52–55, 68–73
  competency trap, 50
  critical dialogue, 60–63, 65
  crucial connections, 63–65
  curiosity, 58, 72–74
  double-loop learning, *54*, 54–55, 69, 73
  embracing, 66–69, 73–74
  ladder of inference, *69*, 69–72, 74
  seeking meaning, 57–60
  self as an instrument, 56–57
  sensemaking attributes, 57–60
  social constructivism, 52–53
  stubbornness, 51–52
  types of, 49
adult learning, viii, xiv, xix–xx, 2, 6, *6*, 36, 98, 144
  andragogy theory, 16
  corporate value, 107
  Kolb's experiential learning cycle, 27–30, *28*
  learning motivation, 16–17
  organizational learning, 113
  principles of, 17
  reflective practice, 27
Advanced Consulting (Pasmore), 99
AE (active experimentation), 28, *28*
after-action reviews, 42, 47
ambiguity. *See also* ambiguity mindset
  ability to embrace group dynamics when faced with, xviii
  capacity for learning through, vii–viii
  defined, xiii
  examples of, xi–xiii
  increasing complexity and, 1
  as learning experience, 91–98
  personal ambiguity story, xi, 143
  in the present, vii
  research questions, xx–xxi, 150–154
  seeking, 88, 152
  sources of, 1–2
  spectrum of comfort with, xiii, xix, 75–76
ambiguity mindset, viii, 1–22
  adaptable mental models, 49–74
  applying, xxi–xxii
  barriers to implementing strategies, 144
  comfort in the unknown, 75–98
  complex adaptive systems, 12–15
  critical reflection, 2, 23–47
  decoding principles, xxi, 3–4
  defined, 2
  developing, 2, 20
  harnessing strategic power of diverse networks, 123–141
  leadership legacy, 148–150
  learning from experience, 15–19
  learning from person, context, and environment, 99–122
  model of, 6, *6*, 165
  objective of, xxi, 2
  research questions, xx–xxi, 150–154
  self-assessment questionnaire, 20–22, 144–145, 157–158
  systems thinking, 9–11
  thinking and behavior strategies, xxi
Amy (health care executive), 41, 55, 60, 64, 88, 92–94, 117–118, 137
analogies, 9, 41, 83, 91
analytical thinking (reductionism), 10–11
andragogy theory, 16
Argyris, Chris, 32, 54, 61, 69, 72, 112
assumptions. *See* challenging assumptions

B

Beer Distribution Game, 84–86
behavior and thinking architecture, learning, xxi, 3, 42, 163. *See also* decoding principles

behavior strategies, 164
  barriers to implementing, 144–148
  challenging assumptions, 35–37, 93–98,
    95–96, 152
  communities of practice, 137–139, 141
  critical dialogue, 60–63, 65
  crucial connections, 63–65
  cultural understanding, 115–119, 122
  exposure to alternative ways of thinking,
    92–93, 98
  insight from differences, 119–121
  ladder of inference, *69*, 69–72, 74
  mind mapping, 108–113, *110*, 122
  organizational learning, 113–115, 121
  reflection in/on action, 40–42
  reflective journaling, 42–47
  seeking ambiguity, 88, 152
  seeking meaning, 57–60
  sensemaking attributes, 57–60
  simulations, 84–86
  social network building, 133–135, *134*, 141
  strategic learning, 127–128, 140–141
  strategic queries, 86–88
  360° reviews, 33–35, 46
being present, 82
B = f(P, E), 99–100, 121, 130
big-picture view, xxi, 3, 20, 52, 64, 102, 146,
  163
Bronfenbrenner, Urie, 4–5
Brooks, Lisa, 43
Budner, Stanley, 21
Built to Change (Lawler and Worley), 130
Burke, W. Warner, 105–106

C

Carter (manager), 12–13, 18–19, 39, 68–69,
  80
CAS. *See* complex adaptive systems
causal mental models, 49
cause-effect mind mapping exercise, 108–113,
  110
CE (concrete experience), 28, *28*
Center for Creative Leadership (CCL), 43,
  108, 149
challenging assumptions
  adaptable mental models, 52–55, 68–73
  comfort in the unknown, 93–98
  critical reflection, 35–37
changing agents, 9, 117, 125
Charlie (renewable energy executive), 30–31,
  36–37, 42, 59–63, 65, 91, 94, 115

Chilean mine collapse, 101–102
Chrisomalis, Caridad Vivian, 100
chronosystem, 4
clarifying behaviors, 18
Clubhouse app, 138
coaching
  being present, 82
  B = f(P, E), 100
  experience of IT department manager,
    66–68
  experience of surgeon, 24
  as important influencers, 93
  leadership, 148
  mental models, 74
  perceptions of time, 148–149
  reflective journaling, 43
  subject-object theory, 39
coalition building, 139–140
cognitive bias, 27, 146
cognitive complexities, xiv, 2, 75
cognitive development theory, 52
Collins, Jim, 149
Columbia University, xiv, 43, 79, 94, 149
Columbia University Business School, 87,
  115
Columbia University Teachers College, 105
comfort in the unknown, 75–98, 144, 164
  analogies, 83
  challenging assumptions, 93–98, *95–96*,
    152
  demystifying the unknown, 80–84
  different spheres of experiences, 89–91
  emotional intelligence, 80–81
  emotional triggers, 80
  exposure to alternative ways of thinking,
    92–93, 98
  knowledge gaps, 76–79
  learning from experience, 90–91
  scan of the senses, 92
  seeking ambiguity, 88, 152
  simulations, 84–86
  strategic queries, 86–88
communities of practice, 64, 137–139, 141
  defined, 137
  social participation, 137–138
competency trap, 50
complex adaptive systems (CAS), 3–4, 12–15,
  163
  cause-effect events, 14
  changing agents, 9, 117, 125
  critical dialogue, 60
  defined, 12

examples of, 12
interconnections and interrelationships, 1,
    6, 10, 19, 53, 88, 104–105
nonlinear relationships, 12, 110, 124
perceptions of time, 147
rapid and dynamic shifts, 13, 55, 137
seeking to control elements within, 117
self-organization, 65
sensemaking, 59
short-term thinking, 14
understanding versus controlling, 12–13
unintended consequences, 13–14
concrete experience (CE), 28, *28*
context, learning through. *See* learn-
    ing through person, context, and
    environment
Cornell University, 4, 27
Covey, Stephen, 149
COVID-19 pandemic, 103, 124, 131, 143
creating meaning, 30–31
critical dialogue, 60–63, 65, 91, 117
critical inquiry, 15, 62
critical reflection, viii, 2, 23–47, 144, 164
    challenging assumptions, 35–37
    creating meaning, 30–31
    defined, 23–24
    deliberately pausing for, 27–30, 46
    disorienting dilemmas, 36
    during and after experimental action, 84
    exploring thinking patterns, 7–8
    hidden barriers to, 25–27
    Kolb's experiential learning cycle, 27–30,
        28
    learning from experience, 15–16
    on mental models, 7
    multiplying versus diminishing talent, 35
    performance coaches, 24–25
    reflection in/on action, 40–42
    reflective journaling, 42–47
    self-awareness, 32–33
    subject-object theory, 38–40, 46
    360° reviews, 33–35, 46
crucial connections, 9, 63–65
cultural understanding, 115–119, 122, 132
curiosity, 58–59, 72–74, 122, 147

D

Daniel (education executive), 12, 92–93
David (academic executive), 117
Dawkins, Monique, 43

decoding principles, xxi, 2–4, 22, 68, 143,
    153, 163
    behavior and thinking architecture, learn-
        ing, xxi, 3, 42, 163
    lack of motivation as barrier to, 104
    unfamiliar experiences, learning from, xx,
        3–4, 76, 96, 152, 163
    wide-angle-lens view, xxi, 3, 20, 52, 64,
        102, 146, 163
demystifying the unknown, 80–84
developing comfort in the unknown. *See*
    comfort in the unknown
development ecology model, 5, *5*
Dewey, John, xi, 15, 62
disambiguating stress, 146–147
diverse networks. *See* harnessing strategic
    power of diverse networks
double-loop learning, *54*, 54–55, 69, 73
Drath, Wilfred H., 108
dress color Internet disagreement, 119–120
Dunning, David, 27
Dunning-Kruger effect, 27
Dutch climate change lawsuit, 131–132
dynamic interactions, 3

E

Ebbinghaus's forgetting curve, 26
ecological systems theory, 4–5
Edmondson, Amy, 102
ego, unmasking, 145–146
emotional intelligence, 35, 80–81, 147
environment, learning through. *See* learn-
    ing through person, context, and
    environment
environment macro sphere, 3, 46, 55, 60, 68,
    93, *96*, 96–97, 103, 121, 123, 132, 153,
    160. *See also* spheres of insight
Eraut, Michael, 113
Eurich, Tasha, 26
Eurich Group, 26
Everyday Negotiation (Kolb and Williams),
    139
executive coaches. *See* coaching
executive interviews, xix–xx. *See also names of*
    specific executives and topics
    academic history, 90
    demographic attributes, 89
    learning from experience, 90
    mental model shifts, 89–90
    types of experiences, 95–97, *95–96*
exosystem, 4, *5*

experience, learning from. *See* learning from experience

experiential learning, xiv–xvii

exposure to alternative ways of thinking, 92–93, 98, 152

Extreme Teaming (Edmondson and Harvey), 102

F

Facebook, xiv, 119

Facilitating Learning with the Adult Brain in Mind (Taylor and Marienau), 83

feedback. *See also* coaching
  adaptive mental models, 73
  brain and, 83
  double-loop learning, 54
  lack of, 27, 35
  receptivity to, 100
  seeking, 27, 105–106, 146
  360° reviews, 33–34

feedback loops, 3, 19
  behavior of the system, 87
  cause-effect mind mapping exercise, 109–110
  critical dialogue, 60
  curiosity and continuous learning, 58–59
  high turnover, 14
  positive versus negative, 10
  purpose of, 10–11
  unintended consequences, 14

"The Fine Line between Stubbornness and Stupidity" (Kets de Vries), 51

The Five Dysfunctions of a Team (Lencioni), 149

Forrester, Jay, 84

Fourth Industrial Revolution, vii

Frenkel-Brunswik, Else, 75–76

Freud, Sigmund, 145

G

gamification, 84–86

Gawande, Atul, 24–25

Gilligan, Carol, 53

Gironda, Linda, 118

Good to Great (Collins), 149

Grant, Adam, 149

group asset networks, 130

group relations conference, xiv–xvii

H

Haj-Yahia, Muhammad M., 28

harnessing strategic power of diverse networks, 123–141, 144, 152, 164
  communities of practice, 137–139, 141
  internal coalitions and department cross-collaboration, 139–140
  knowledge sharing, 128–131, 140
  seeking diverse stakeholder insights, 131–133
  situated learning, 135–137
  social network building, 133–135, *134*, 141
  strategic assumptions, 124–127
  strategic learning, 127–128, 140–141
  wicked problems, 124–127

Harvard Business School, 32

Harvard Law School, 139

Harvard University, 7, 43, 108

Harvey, Jean-Francois, 102

Hazel (entrepreneurial executive), 42, 58, 63, 134–135

holism. *See* systems thinking

Holland, John Henry, 12, 113

How Diversity Makes Us Smarter (Phillips), 115

I

ideal self versus actual self, 32

If Only We Knew What We Know (O'Dell and Grayson), 113

illusion of control, 145–146

individual macro sphere, 3, 55, 60, 68, 93, *96*, 96–97, 103, 121, 123, 153, 159. *See also* spheres of insight

informal learning, 15, 17, 55, 78, 90, 98, 114, 131, 135–136, 138, 152–153

Ingersoll, Richard, 130

Ingham, Harry, 33

initiating behaviors, 18

In Over Our Heads (Kegan), 38

INSEAD, 43, 149

insight from differences, 119–121

interconnections and interrelationships, 1, 6, 10, 19, 53, 88, 104–105

International Coaching Federation, 82

Intolerance of Ambiguity assessment, 21

Isabella (executive), 51–52

J

Johari window communication model, 32–33, *33*, 146
journaling. *See* reflective journaling
Journal of Vision, 119

K

Kahneman, Daniel, 93, 149
Karim (information and technology executive), 31, 41, 55–56, 59, 62–63, 94
Kegan, Robert, 7, 38
Kelman, Herbert C., 108
Kets de Vries, Manfred, 51–52
Kim (manager), 70–71
knowledge gaps, 1, 76–79
    awareness of, 114
    communication mechanisms, 78
    corporate connectors, 77
    employees in isolation, 77
    informal learning, 78
    knowledge-sharing behaviors, 78
    learning from experience, 76–77
    social network analysis, 133–134
    soft power issues, 107
knowledge sharing, 62, 78, 112–113, 125, 128–131, 138, 140
Knowles, Malcolm, 16
Kolb, David, 15, 27–29
Kolb, Deborah, 139
Kolb's experiential learning cycle, 27–30, *28*
Kruger, Justin, 27
Krumboltz, John, 59
Kubberod, Elin, 136

L

ladder of inference, *69*, 69–72, 146
    adopting beliefs, 71
    drawing conclusions, 70–71
    making assumptions, 70
    not racing to top of, 71–72, 74
    selecting observable data, 70
    taking action, 71
    unmasking ego, 146
Lave, Jean, 64, 135, 138
Leadership (Northouse), 148
leadership legacy, 148–150
    defined, 150
    gradual, deliberate process, 149
    leadership, defined, 148
    research and courses, 149

Lean In (Sandberg), xiv
learning agility, 104–107, 122
    defined, 105
    determinants of, 106
"Learning and Supervisory Styles in the Training of Social Workers" (Wolfsfeld and Haj-Yahia), 28
learning from experience, xiv, 3, 15–20, 76–77, 90–91, 163
    Beer Distribution Game, 84–86
    components of, 15
    creating meaning, 30–31
    critical inquiry, 62
    default communication behaviors, 18
    defined, 15
    disambiguating stress, 147
    emotional intelligence, 80–81
    experiential learning versus, 15
    Kolb's experiential learning cycle, 27–30, *28*
    learning motivation, 16–17
    principles of adult learning, 17
    reflection in/on action, 40–42
    social and situational context, 135–137
    social constructivism, 52–53
    unmasking ego, 146
learning through person, context, and environment, 99–122, 130, 144, 152, 164
    $B = f(P, E)$, 99–100
    cultural understanding, 115–119, 122
    extreme teaming, 102
    feedback receptivity, 100
    insight from differences, 119–121
    learning agility, 104–107, 122
    mind mapping, 108–113, *110*, 122
    motivational theories, 104–107
    organizational learning, 113–115, 121
    social intelligence, 103–104
    soft power issues, 107–108
    understanding all spheres of insight, 101–103
Lencioni, Patrick, 149
Leonardo (private equity executive), 78, 105
lessons-learned activities, 86, 109, 146
Levin, Al, 59
Lewin, Kurt, 99, 130, 151
Lewis Levin, Kameron, 130–131
logical mental models, 49
London School of Economics, 126
Louis, Meryl Reis, 57
Luc (transportation executive), 116–117, 135
Luft, Joseph, 33

"lunch and learn" sessions, 77
Lynn (health care executive), 80, 82

M

macrosystem, 4, *5*
Marcus (shipping executive), 40–41, 64–65,
    92, 114–116, 136
Marienau, Catherine, 83
Marwan (conglomerate executive), 132
McGill University, 61
McKeown, Greg, 35, 149
meaning
    creating, 30–31
    seeking, 57–60, 151
Men Are from Mars, Women Are from Venus
    (Gray), 93
mental models, 3, 7–8, 20, 89, 163. *See also*
    adaptable mental models
    assumptions, 70–73
    B = *f*(P, E), 99–100
    defined, 7
    emotional intelligence, 80–81
    exploring thinking patterns, 7–8
    metacognition, 8
    reflection, 50
    sensemaking attributes, 57–60
    social constructivism, 52–53
    worldview approach, 50
Merton, Robert K., 13
mesosystem, 4
metacognition, 8
Mezirow, Jack, 23, 36
Michael (hospitality investment executive),
    62, 64–65, 88, 91–92, 104, 113–114,
    118
microsystem, 4, *5*
microteams, 137
Milliken, Frances, 58
mindfulness, 13, 52, 82
mind mapping, 108–113, *110*, 122
    elements, people, influencers present at
        learning moment, 111
    perceptions and beliefs about unexpected
        changes, 111
    perceptions of time, 148
    significant learning moments, 111
    thinking strategies, 112
    understanding ambiguity, 110–111
Mintzberg, Henry, 61
MIT (Massachusetts Institute of Technol-
    ogy), 32, 84–85

MIT Sloan School of Management, 15
model of inference, 49
model theory of deduction, 49
motivational theories, 104–107
Multipliers (Wiseman and McKeown), 35,
    149
"My Dinner Party" exercise, 50–51, 161–162

N

need-to-know category, 128
network of learning relationships, 64–65
NeuroLeadership Institute, 82
neuroscience
    demystifying the unknown, 82–83
    hidden barriers to critical reflection, 26
New Yorker, 24
New York University, 53, 119
Nicolaides, Aliki, 79–80
nonlinear relationships, 12, 110, 124
Northouse, Peter, 148
Norwegian School of Entrepreneurship, 136
Noumair, Debra A., xiv

O

open systems, 6, 20
organizational behavior theories, xiv, 2, 6, *6*,
    57, 108, 140, 144
organizational learning, 62, 97, 113–115, 121,
    145
organizational psychology, xiv, xix–xx, 105
organization macro sphere, 3, 46, 55, 60, 68,
    93, *96*, 96–97, 103, 121, 123, 132, 153,
    160. *See also* spheres of insight
Osteen, Dr., 24–25
overconfidence bias, 26–27
Owen, Renee, 36

P

paradox of synchronicity, 118
Pasmore, Bill, 99–100
passive learning, 80
Penn State University, 9
perceptions of time, 147–148
"Personal Best" (Gawande), 24–25
person, learning through. *See* learn-
    ing through person, context, and
    environment
perspective-taking skills, 3
perturbation, 34
Pettersen, Inger Beate, 136

Phillips, Katherine W., 115
Piaget, Jean, 52
Pietersen, Willie, 87, 127
planned happenstance learning theory, 59
PLOS, 26
process behaviors, 18

R

Rachid (oil and gas executive), 31, 55, 59, 65, 107, 136
rapid and dynamic shifts, 13, 55, 137
reacting behaviors, 18
reasoning under uncertainty, 49
reflection. *See* critical reflection
reflection in/on action, 40–42, 146
reflective journaling, 42–47, 80
    defined, 43
    examples of, 42–43
    prompts for, 44–45, 159–160
    research into, 43–44
    unmasking ego, 146
reflective observation (RO), 28, *28*
Rehman, Aamir A., 28–29
Richmond, Barry, 9
Rittel, Horst, 124–125
Robert (executive), 66–68, 94
Rock, David, 82
Rosati, Pamela Booth, 17–18
Rosenhead, Jonathan, 126

S

safety huddle practice, 41
Sandberg, Sheryl, xiv
Santiago (manager), 16
Schön, Donald, 32, 40–41, 54, 61, 84
secular spiritual pedagogical practices, 36
seeking ambiguity, 88, 152
seeking meaning, 57–60, 151
self as an instrument, 56–57
self-assessment questionnaire, 20–22, 144–145, 157–158
self-awareness, 32–33, 35, 82, 146
    ideal self versus actual self, 32
    Johari window communication model, 32–33, *33*
self-organization, 65
self-reflection. *See* critical reflection
Senge, Peter, 114
sensemaking attributes, 57–60, 151
Sensemaking in Organizations (Weick), 57

The 7 Habits of Highly Effective People (Covey), 149
short-term thinking, 3
simulations, 84–86
situated learning
    ambiguous, 135–137
    communities of practice, 64, 137–139
social and situational context, 135–137
social constructivism, 52–53, 84, 103–104
social influence theory, 108
social intelligence, 103–104, 122, 128, 137, 148
social network analysis (SNA), 133–135, *134*, 141
soft power issues, 107–108
Southern Oregon University, 36
spheres of insight, 4–6, 163
    building cognitive intellectual capacity, 153
    comfort in the unknown, 76, 82, 86, 89, 93, *96*, 96–98
    harnessing strategic power of diverse networks, 123, 128, 137, 141
    learning through person, context, and environment, 103, 107, 121
    mental models, 52–53, 55, 60, 68
    reflective journaling prompts, 159–160
    unmasking ego, 145
Stanford University, 59
Starbuck, William, 58
Stasser, Garold, 129
strategic assumptions, 124–127
strategic learning, xxii, 4, 97, 127–128, 140–141, 152–153
Strategic Learning (Pietersen), 87, 127
strategic queries, 86–88
stubbornness, 51–52
subject-object theory, 38–40, 46, 147
synthesis. *See* systems thinking
systems structure, 9
systems thinking, xiv, xx, 2–3, 6, *6*, 9–12, 19, 88, 126, 144, 146, 163
    analytical thinking versus, 10–11
    car analogy, 9
    communities of practice, 138
    critical dialogue, 61
    defined, 9
    dynamic behavior, 9–10
    emotional intelligence, 80–81
    feedback loops, 10–11
    interactions within system, 110

open systems, 6
systems structure, 9
whole rather than parts, 10
worldview approach, 10

T

Taylor, Kathleen, 82–83
Thailand cave incident, 102–103
Think Again (Grant), 149
Thinking, Fast and Slow (Kahneman), 93, 149
thinking strategies
  barriers to implementing, 144–148
  B = *f*(P, E), 99–100
  challenging self-assumptions, 52–55,
    68–73
  creating meaning, 30–31
  demystifying the unknown, 80–84
  double-loop learning, *54*, 54–55, 69, 73
  emotional intelligence, 80–81
  knowing gaps, 76–79
  knowledge sharing, 128–131, 140
  learning agility, 104–107, 122
  motivational theories, 104–107
  self-awareness, 32–33
  social constructivism, 52–53
  social intelligence, 103–104
  strategic assumptions, 124–127
  subject-object theory, 38–40, 46
  wicked problems, 124–127
Thorndike, Edward Lee, 105
thought leaders, 92–94, 149
360° reviews, 33–35, 46
Titus, William, 129
Tuckman's theory of teams, xvii

U

UAE. *See* United Arab Emirates
Uber, 112
UCLA (University of California, Los Angeles), 57
unfamiliar experiences, learning from, xx, 3–4,
  76, 96, 152, 163
unintended consequences, 3
  cause-effect events, 14
  examples of, 13–14
  perverse results, 13
  types of, 13
  unexpected benefits, 13
  unexpected drawbacks, 13

United Arab Emirates (UAE), xix–xx
  cultural differences, 116–117, 132
  expatriate executives, 89
  systems thinking approach to education,
    12
University of California, Berkeley, 124
University of California, Los Angeles
  (UCLA), 57
University of Michigan, 12
University of Pennsylvania, 130
Urgenda Foundation, 132

V

Vogt, Eric, 79
VUCA (volatility, uncertainty, complexity,
  and ambiguity) environments, vii, 87,
  127
Vygotsky, Lev, 53

W

Wallisch, Pascal, 119–120
Weatherhead School of Management, 15
Webber, Melvin, 124–125
Weick, Karl, 57
Wenger, Etienne, 64, 135, 138
whole rather than parts, 10, 12, 19, 87
wicked problems, 124–127
  characteristics of, 125–126
  criteria for dealing with, 126–127
  defined, 124
wide-angle-lens (big-picture) view, xxi, 3, 20,
  52, 64, 102, 146, 163
Williams, Judith, 139
Wiseman, Liz, 35, 149
Wolfsfeld, Lauren, 28
work-life balance, 9
worldview approach, 31, 36, 50, 73, 89, 108,
  138
  double-loop learning, 54
  social constructivism, 104
  subject-object theory, 38
  systems thinking, 10
  wide-angle-lens view, 102

Y

Yorks, Lyle, 79–80

ABOUT THE AUTHOR

DR. DEBBIE SUTHERLAND is an academic executive with over twenty years of global work experiences in Canada, Southeast Asia, Europe, and the Middle East. She is continually learning about the dynamics and hidden power of adult learning, organizational behaviors, and systems thinking through the business lens. She has worked in a variety of centralized roles in complex adaptive systems and international start-up organizations and is currently living and working as an executive in the UAE. She specializes in setting up the ideal structure, culture, and people-centric programs to enable leaders to thrive in the workplace. Debbie has completed her doctorate of education in adult and organizational learning and an executive master's degree in socio-organizational psychology, each from Columbia University, and is a certified executive coach.